Social Issues in Literature

Wilderness Adventure in Jon Krakauer's *Into the Wild*

Other Books in the Social Issues in Literature Series:

Social Issues
in Literature

Wilderness Adventure in Jon Krakauer's *Into the Wild*

Noël Merino, Book Editor

GREENHAVEN PRESS
A part of Gale, Cengage Learning

GALE
CENGAGE Learning·

Farmington Hills, Mich • San Francisco • New York • Waterville, Maine
Meriden, Conn • Mason, Ohio • Chicago

Elizabeth Des Chenes, *Director, Content Strategy*
Douglas Dentino, *Manager, New Product*

For more information, contact:
Greenhaven Press
27500 Drake Rd.
Farmington Hills, MI 48331-3535
Or you can visit our Internet site at gale.cengage.com

Articles in Greenhaven Press anthologies are often edited for length to meet page requirements. In addition, original titles of these works are changed to clearly present the main thesis and to explicitly indicate the author's opinion. Every effort is made to ensure that Greenhaven Press accurately reflects the original intent of the authors. Every effort has been made to trace the owners of copyrighted material.

Cover image © Jurgen Frank/Corbis.

LIBRARY OF CONGRESS CATALOGING-IN-PUBLICATION DATA

Wilderness Adventure in Jon Krakauer's Into the Wild / Noël Merino, book editor.
    pages cm. -- (Social Issues in Literature)
    Summary: "This series brings together the disciplines of sociology and literature. It looks at a work of literature through the lens of the major social issue that is reflected in it"-- Provided by publisher.
    Includes bibliographical references and index.
    ISBN 978-0-7377-6976-0 (hardback) -- ISBN 978-0-7377-6977-7 (paperback)
    1. Krakauer, Jon--Criticism and interpretation. 2. American literature--20th century--History and criticism. 3. Mountaineering in literature. 4. Outdoor life in literature. I. Merino, Noël, editor.
    PS3561.R238Z93 2015
    814'.54--dc23
                             2014015789

Printed in the United States of America
2 3 4 5 6   19 18 17 16 15

Contents

Krakauer tells the story of Christopher McCandless in a way that portrays him as a heroic adventurer, using passages from McCandless's favorite authors, as well as from authors of Krakauer's choosing.

Introduction

The publication of Jon Krakauer's nonfiction *Into the Wild* has garnered fans and critics alike and continues to be a polarizing book that has enjoyed immense popularity. Christopher (Chris) McCandless went into the Alaskan wilderness in April 1992 after living on the road for two years under the pseudonym Alexander Supertramp. In September 1992, McCandless's dead body was found inside an abandoned bus. Writer and mountain climber Krakauer became interested in McCandless's death and published an article for *Outside* magazine about the hermit's demise in January 1993, after conducting research on the months leading up to McCandless's trip into the wilderness. The article became a springboard for the book *Into the Wild*.

Into the Wild was published in 1996 and spent more than two years on the *New York Times* best-sellers list. Krakauer's account of McCandless's life garnered even more recognition after the release of the 2007 film of the same name, directed by Sean Penn with input from Krakauer. McCandless's story has been controversial for several reasons, with some objecting to the life choices made by McCandless and others objecting to the story's retelling by Krakauer.

Fans and critics of McCandless's lifestyle see him as either a kind of hero or a kind of selfish fool, respectively. For fans of McCandless, his venture on the road and into the wilderness while taking few personal belongings is a pilgrimage worthy of praise, a trip to be celebrated for the hiker's courage and authenticity, despite his ultimate death. For McCandless's detractors, his journey is one of selfish cruelty toward his family and friends, a journey they disapprove of due to his naïve and foolish decisions that led to his unnecessary death.

For Krakauer, too, there are fans and critics. Fans see Krakauer as having taken an unsympathetic protagonist and molding him into a more human character by attempting to explain the internal motivation for his journey, partly by relating McCandless's story to his own life story. Critics, though, see Krakauer as romanticizing the harmful choices of an overly confident young man who rejected the love and kindness of those around him.

It must be remembered that Krakauer's account of the life of McCandless is the author's version, and there is considerable debate over several of Krakauer's speculations about McCandless's life and death. Since the publication of Krakauer's book, there has never been a consensus about the ultimate cause of McCandless's passing. In his 1993 article for *Outside*, Krakauer first speculated that McCandless had mistakenly consumed toxic wild sweet pea seeds instead of wild potato seeds, ultimately causing his death. This hypothesis turned out to be flawed, prompting Krakauer to speculate in *Into the Wild* that McCandless had eaten wild potato seeds that contained a toxic alkaloid. Responding to scientists' criticism of that theory, Krakauer once again revised his theory in 2013, speculating in an article in the *New Yorker* that McCandless died from a neurotoxin, beta-N-oxalyl-L-alpha-beta diaminopropionic acid (ODAP), present in the wild potato seeds eaten by McCandless. In that article, Krakauer wrote, "Considering that potentially crippling levels of ODAP are found in wild-potato seeds, and given the symptoms McCandless described and attributed to the wild-potato seeds he ate, there is ample reason to believe that McCandless contracted lathyrism from eating those seeds."

For Krakauer, controversy has never been a reason to shy away from writing a story. His 1997 book, *Into Thin Air: A Personal Account of the Mt. Everest Disaster*, garnered disapproval from many climbers for his account of an ascent on Mount Everest that resulted in several deaths. His 2003 book, *Under the Banner of Heaven: A Story of Violent Faith*, created controversy for allegedly portraying Mormons in a negative light.

If there is one point of agreement among fans and critics of Krakauer's *Into the Wild*, it is that the story of McCandless is a compelling one. Why has this young man who ended up dead in the wilderness captured the attention of so many people worldwide? What does this fascination say about our view of the wilderness and the human relationship to it? Should McCandless's wilderness adventure be viewed as heroic, foolish, or simply uninteresting? Does Krakauer's interest in and description of McCandless's life say more about the author or more about McCandless? Answers to these questions and others are explored and debated in *Social Issues in Literature: Wilderness Adventure in Jon Krakauer's* Into the Wild.

Chronology

1954
Krakauer is born April 12 in Brookline, Massachusetts.

1956 or 1957
Krakauer's family moves to Corvallis, Oregon.

1962 or 1963
Krakauer's father introduces him to mountaineering.

1976
Krakauer graduates from Hampshire College in Amherst, Massachusetts, with a degree in environmental studies.

1977
Krakauer attempts to summit Devils Thumb in southeastern Alaska.

1980
Krakauer marries climber Linda Mariam Moore.

1983
Krakauer quits his building job in Boulder, Colorado, to focus on writing.

1990
Eiger Dreams: Ventures Among Men and Mountains is published.

1993
Krakauer writes an article about Chris McCandless's death for *Outside*.

1996
Into the Wild is published.

1996

Krakauer climbs Mount Everest and four of his climbing companions die.

1997

Into Thin Air: A Personal Account of the Mt. Everest Disaster is published.

2003

Under the Banner of Heaven: A Story of Violent Faith is published.

2007

The film version of *Into the Wild*, directed by Sean Penn, is released.

2009

Where Men Win Glory: The Odyssey of Pat Tillman is published.

2011

Three Cups of Deceit: How Greg Mortenson, Humanitarian Hero, Lost His Way is published as an e-book and later in paperback format.

CHAPTER 1

Background on
Jon Krakauer

The Life of Jon Krakauer

UXL Biographies

UXL Biographies *is a collection of biographies of historic and contemporary people from a variety of professions and a wide range of nationalities and ethnic groups.*

In the following biographical essay, UXL Biographies *portrays the life of writer Jon Krakauer, recounting the author's early years and describing how he became a writer.* UXL Biographies *describes the content of Krakauer's six nonfiction books:* Eiger Dreams: Ventures Among Men and Mountains; Into the Wild; Into Thin Air: A Personal Account of the Mt. Everest Disaster; Under the Banner of Heaven: A Story of Violent Faith; Where Men Win Glory: The Odyssey of Pat Tillman; *and* Three Cups of Deceit: How Greg Mortenson, Humanitarian Hero, Lost His Way. UXL Biographies *notes that several of Krakauer's titles have been best sellers and that his writing has won awards, though his subject matter has not been free of controversy.*

Jon Krakauer is a highly acclaimed, award-winning author who is known primarily for his captivating, true-life stories about the outdoors and mountain climbing. The award-winning writer first made a name for himself as a writer and contributing editor for *Outside* magazine. Krakauer—who had no formal training as a writer—eventually was able to leave his work as a carpenter and fisherman in the early 1980s to pursue writing full time as a freelance writer. Drawing on his real-life experiences as a carpenter, fisherman, and avid outdoorsman, his articles soon were appearing in a number of other publications like *Smithsonian* and *National Geographic*

"Jon Krakauer," *UXL Biographies*. Detroit: U*X*L, 2011. Copyright © 2011 Cengage Learning.

magazine. As he once told *Outside Online*: "I have never received any formal training as a writer. Whenever I read something that moves me, I re-read it many times to try and figure out how its author has worked his or her magic. . . . Like any craft, the longer and harder you work at your writing, the more likely you are to get better at it."

After experiencing success writing for magazines, Krakauer started to turn his attention toward writing books. He has since written several nonfiction best sellers, including *Into the Wild* (1996), *Into Thin Air* (1997), *Under the Banner of Heaven* (2003), and *Where Men Win Glory: The Odyssey of Pat Tillman* (2009). He also wrote an e-book in 2011 called *Three Cups of Deceit*.

The Early Years

Krakauer was born on April 12, 1954, in Brookline, Massachusetts, to his father, Lewis (a physician), and his mother, Linda (an art teacher). While growing up in Corvallis, Oregon, Krakauer's father introduced him to mountaineering when he was eight years old, sparking a lifelong interest in the pursuit. His father also was acquainted with Willi Unsoeld, who was part of the first American expedition to Mount Everest in 1963. Krakauer grew up idolizing Unsoeld and climber Tom Hornbein, holding onto a dream that he, too, would one day ascend to the top of Mount Everest.

In the 1970s, Krakauer began attending Hampshire College in Amherst, Massachusetts, and graduated in 1976 with a degree in environmental studies. While attending college, Krakauer met David Roberts—a writer also interested in climbing who shared stories about the excellent climbing in Alaska. As Krakauer told *People* magazine, "I became a climbing bum. I worked as a carpenter in Boulder, Colorado, five months of the year, climbed the rest." In 1974, he went to Alaska and climbed the previously unexplored Alaskan Arri-

Jon Krakauer is an American author and mountain climber whose writings focus primarily on the outdoors. © Rex Rystedt/The LIFE Images Collection/Getty Images.

getch Peaks in the Brooks Range. Following his successful climb, the American Alpine Club asked Krakauer to write about his experience, providing him with his first opportunity to write about his mountain-climbing experiences. He followed that article three years later with one about another climbing experience in the British magazine *Mountain*. The latter article and the pay he received from it convinced Krakauer that he was able to financially support himself as a writer rather than continue working as a carpenter and commercial fisherman. So in 1983, Krakauer quit his job as foreman of a house-building crew to pursue writing as a full-time career.

Articles About Climbing

Though he never received any formal training as a writer, Krakauer made it a practice of studying writing; he liked to figure out how others worked their magic through the written word. He also successfully mined his own real-life experiences and began querying magazine editors to try to interest them in his story ideas. Krakauer's efforts paid off, and he soon was making enough money to pay the bills through his writing. His stories soon were appearing in a number of well-regarded national publications like *Outside, Architectural Digest, Smithsonian, National Geographic,* and *Rolling Stone.*

Krakauer also published his first book, *Eiger Dreams: Ventures Among Men and Mountains,* in 1990. The book pulled together a collection of magazine articles that Krakauer had written for *Outside* and *Smithsonian.* In the articles throughout the book, Krakauer told of countless climbing experiences, including his ascents of Mount McKinley and the North Face of the Eiger in Switzerland. Through the storytelling in his book, Krakauer also addressed the question of why anyone would want to risk life and limb climbing such high mountain peaks. In the *New York Times Book Review,* Tim Cahill wrote that Krakauer's "... snow-capped peaks set against limitless blue skies present problems that inspire irrefutable human experiences: fear and triumph, damnation and salvation. There is beauty in his mountains beyond that expressed in conventional sermons. His reverence is earned, and it's entirely genuine."

The Story of Chris McCandless

Then in the early 1990s, *Outside* magazine asked Krakauer to write a story about a bright young man by the name of Chris McCandless from Washington, D.C., who ventured into the Alaskan wilderness on a spiritual quest, only to lose his life. Inspired by the writings of Leo Tolstoy, the twenty-four-year-old honors graduate decided to get rid of all his possessions and venture into the wilderness to experience transcendence. Renaming himself Alex Supertramp, McCandless wandered through the American West, eventually reaching Alaska, where he hiked into the bush near Denali National Park [and Preserve] with plans to live off the land. But only four months later, his decomposing body was discovered by a group of moose hunters. McCandless had starved to death. Krakauer was able to successfully reconstruct the last two years of the young man's life from McCandless's journals and postcards, as well as through interviews with those who knew him, to write the *Outside* magazine article.

One year after the *Outside* article appeared about McCandless, Krakauer still found himself gripped by the young man's story and began to write *Into the Wild* (1996), which became Krakauer's first best seller. In the introduction of the book, Krakauer wrote: "I was haunted by the particulars of the boy's starvation and by vague, unsettling parallels between events in his life and those in my own." Much like McCandless, Krakauer had traveled to Alaska while in his twenties to climb Devils Thumb against the advice of family and friends who thought it was a foolhardy expedition on a dangerous peak. "The fact that I survived my Alaskan adventure and McCandless did not survive his was largely a matter of chance," Krakauer wrote, adding that he ". . . couldn't resist stealing up to the edge of doom and peering over the brink. The view into that swirling black vortex terrified me, but I caught sight of something elemental in that shadowy glimpse, some forbidden, fascinating riddle." The book—which spent two years on the *New York Times* best-sellers list—was adapted into a film directed by Sean Penn in 2007.

Documenting a Tragic Expedition

Then in May 1996, Krakauer joined an expedition of twenty-three people that climbed Mount Everest. After a request from *Outside* editors to write about the increase in commercialization of Mount Everest climbing expeditions, Krakauer joined an expedition with teams headed up by two of the world's most elite climbers—Rob Hall (c. 1961–1996) of New Zealand and Scott Fischer (c. 1956—1996) of the United States. Hall and Fischer each owned a company that specialized in taking amateur climbers to the Everest summit. The two men were promoting their businesses to potential clients.

The climb to the summit was to be the fulfillment of Krakauer's boyhood dream, but the expedition had a tragic outcome and left him with some unsettling conclusions—one of which was the inexperience of many of the climbers. As he wrote in *Outside*, "There's a lot of people here who shouldn't be here. And maybe I shouldn't be here. . . . People who wouldn't have the time and the experience—but they have the money—can do this." On his way down the peak, Krakauer was unaware that several other climbers were stranded behind him in a sudden winter storm. In the end, eight other climbers—including Hall—died during the ordeal. Haunted by guilt that he was unable to save those who died, Krakauer wrote his article for *Outside*, but wanted to explore the circumstances of the deadly expedition in more depth. The result was Krakauer's book *Into Thin Air: A Personal Account of the Mt. Everest Disaster*, which climbed to the top of the *New York Times* bestsellers list and was translated into more than twenty-five languages. It also was named Book of the Year by *Time* magazine and was one of three finalists for the general nonfiction Pulitzer Prize. The magazine article about the expedition received a National Magazine Award.

Though the book received widespread acclaim, Krakauer received sharp criticism from the family and friends of those who died during the expedition, and also from some of the other climbers who survived the ordeal. Some accused Krakauer of profiting from the tragic circumstances that led to the death of the eight climbers. Krakauer defended himself, saying that he worked hard to present what happened in an "even-handed, sympathetic manner that did not sensationalize the tragedy or cause undue pain to friends and families of the victims."

As a tribute to those lost during the Everest expedition, Krakauer established the Everest '96 Memorial Fund with the Boulder Community Foundation, using proceeds from the sale of *Into Thin Air*. As of 2012, the fund had donated more than $1.7 million to a wide variety of charities, including the American Himalayan Foundation, Educate the Children, and Veterans Helping Veterans Now.

Later Exposé Titles

For his next book, Krakauer delved into religious fundamentalism in *Under the Banner of Heaven: A Story of Violent Faith*, (2003). According to Matthew Flamm in *Entertainment Weekly*, Krakauer said he was drawn to the subject matter because he wanted to understand "the terrible things people do . . . in the name of God." The investigative nonfiction book simultaneously explores the origin and history of the Mormons (Church of Jesus Christ of Latter-day Saints), as well as a double murder committed in the name of God by two fundamentalist Mormon brothers. The book received mixed reviews, with some criticizing Krakauer's failure to highlight some of the positive aspects of the Mormon religion. Two weeks before the publication of *Under the Banner of Heaven*, the Mormon Church released a five-page rebuttal of information cited in the book. Krakauer subsequently defended his work, accusing the church of attempting to whitewash its history.

Krakauer's next book, *Where Men Win Glory: The Odyssey of Pat Tillman* (2009), also was outside of the author's usual subject matter. To research the book, Krakauer spent five months embedded with combat forces along the Afghanistan-Pakistan border. The result was a thoroughly researched account of the life and death of NFL [National Football League] defensive back Pat Tillman. Shortly after the 9/11 attacks [referring to the terrorist attacks on the United States on September 11, 2001], Tillman chose to leave his million-dollar career to become an Army Ranger, along with his brother Kevin. Tillman ultimately lost his life in Afghanistan in 2004. The U.S. Army claimed that he died a hero, but in his book, Krakauer exposed the fact that Tillman died as the result of friendly fire. Krakauer devotes much of the book to exposing the military's efforts to cover up the true cause of Tillman's death. Krakauer's work—particularly the way he exposed the military's cover-up—earned him high praise. In his review of the book in the *New York Times Book Review*, Dexter Filkins wrote: "The biggest problem with *Where Men Win Glory* is that nearly all the drama and import—Tillman's death and the cover-up—are saved for the last hundred pages." But, as Filkins noted, "once Tillman lands in Afghanistan . . . Krakauer's narrative lifts off. The death of Tillman is handled deftly."

Krakauer next published an e-book in 2011 called *Three Cups of Deceit: How Greg Mortenson, Humanitarian Hero, Lost His Way*. Krakauer had previously been a financial supporter of [American humanitarian and former mountaineer Greg] Mortenson's work through the nonprofit Central Asia Institute. But Krakauer became disillusioned with Mortenson and the nonprofit, and began questioning Mortenson's credibility and the financial practices of the nonprofit. Just before his book was published, Krakauer appeared on an April 2011 segment of *60 Minutes* that called Mortenson and his nonprofit into question. The segment mostly outlined the conclusions that Krakauer reached in his book. The end result of the segment and Krakauer's exposé was an investigation into Mortenson and the Central Asia Institute. According to media reports in April 2012, the Montana state attorney general removed Mortenson from the Central Asia Institute and forced him to pay back $1 million. Donor money—which was given to promote education and literacy in Central Asia—was instead spent on charter flights for family vacations, clothing, and Internet downloads. The investigation found that Mortenson's personal wealth grew significantly as his charity became more popular, and that he took speaking fees from the charity for his promotional work. The Montana attorney general's office also found that the charity had spent $4 million since 2006 buying copies of *Three Cups of Tea* (the story of how Mortenson became a humanitarian in Central Asia), and Mortenson's other book, *Stones into Schools*, to give away to libraries and schools as a way to promote its work. The investigation also revealed that the charity spent $5 million advertising the books.

In *Three Cups of Deceit*, Krakauer summed up his view of Mortenson and his charity. "The image of Mortenson that has been created for public consumption is an artifact born of fantasy, audacity, and an apparently insatiable hunger for esteem. Mortenson has lied about the noble deeds he has done, the risks he has taken, the people he has met, the number of schools he has built. *Three Cups of Tea* has much in common with *A Million Little Pieces*, the infamous autobiography by [American writer] James Frey that was exposed as a sham. But Frey, unlike Mortenson, didn't use his phony memoir to solicit tens of millions of dollars in donations from unsuspecting readers, myself among them." Krakauer has donated proceeds from *Three Cups of Deceit* to the Stop Girl Trafficking [program] at the American Himalayan Foundation.

In addition to his best-selling-author status, Krakauer also has won a number of awards for his writing. He received an Academy Award in Literature from the American Academy of Arts and Letters in 1999 for his work. According to the academy, "Krakauer combines the tenacity and courage of the finest tradition of investigative journalism with the stylish subtlety and profound insight of the born writer. His account of an ascent of Mount Everest has led to a general reevaluation of climbing and of the commercialization of what was once a romantic, solitary sport; while his account of the life and death of Christopher McCandless, who died of starvation after challenging the Alaskan wilderness, delves even more deeply and disturbingly into the fascination of nature and the devastating effects of its lure on a young and curious mind." For *Into Thin Air*, Krakauer received an American Library Association Best Books for Young Adults in 1998.

Critics' Responses to Krakauer's Nonfiction Works

Concise Major 21st-Century Writers

Concise Major 21st-Century Writers is a multivolume collection of biographies about authors who are most often studied in college and high school.

In the following viewpoint, Concise Major 21st-Century Writers *recounts the critical reception to four of Krakauer's books. The author contends that Krakauer's portrayal of mountain climbing, in the essays compiled in* Eiger Dreams: Ventures Among Men and Mountains, *was praised for its honesty about the sport.* Concise Major 21st-Century Writers *claims that Krakauer's book about Christopher McCandless,* Into the Wild, *received largely positive appraisals despite the critiques of McCandless himself. The author contends that despite the painful and personal content of* Into Thin Air: A Personal Account of the Mt. Everest Disaster, *critics generally believed the book succeeded.* Concise Major 21st-Century Writers *also asserts that Krakauer's book* Under the Banner of Heaven: A Story of Violent Faith *was perhaps the least well received, due to its controversial subject matter, its departure from the adventure tale formula, and its overly ambitious goals.*

Best known as the author of the gripping 1997 book *Into Thin Air: A Personal Account of the Mt. Everest Disaster,* which describes a mountaineering tragedy, Jon Krakauer is a journalist and nonfiction author whose award-winning writings on mountain climbing and other sports combine the knowledge of the insider with the writer's sense of dramatic and well-timed storytelling. Critics have recommended the

"Krakauer, Jon 1954–," pp. 2069–2072 in *Concise Major 21st-Century Writers,* ed. Tracey L. Matthews, vol. 3. Detroit: Gale, 2006. Copyright © 2006 Cengage Learning.

author's first book-length publication, *Eiger Dreams: Ventures Among Men and Mountains*, a collection of essays on mountain climbing, for armchair adventurers, novices, and experienced climbers alike, praising its thrilling subject matter and Krakauer's unpretentious prose style. Krakauer's second book, *Into the Wild*, reconstructs the last days of Christopher McCandless, a young man who gave away all his possessions and traveled to the Alaskan wilderness only to die of starvation in an abandoned bus. Drawing on numerous interviews, Krakauer paints a touching picture of the troubled young man, while also attempting to understand the motivations for McCandless's trip to one of nature's most forbidding landscapes.

Praise and Criticism of Krakauer's Works

Eiger Dreams is a collection of twelve essays, several featuring famous eccentrics of the mountain-climbing set—including John Gill, who climbs boulders, and the Burgess twins [Adrian and Alan], who, without an income, manage to travel the world climbing its most challenging peaks—while others center on the mountains themselves. The Eiger of the title is a fiercely difficult mountain in Switzerland that the author attempted and failed to climb, providing one of the occasional moments of humor in these adventure-filled pages. "Krakauer conveys well the formidable, even terrifying aspects of the sport," emphasized a reviewer for *Kirkus Reviews*. Tim Cahill, critic for the *New York Times Book Review*, singled out the author's avoidance of the clichés of "conquering" mountain peaks, and the trite epiphanies that occur there: "There is a beauty in his mountains beyond that expressed in conventional sermons. His reverence is earned, and it's entirely genuine."

Krakauer's *Into the Wild* is the nonfiction account of the life and death of McCandless. A brilliant young man from a loving and prosperous family, McCandless abandoned his upper-middle-class existence to live the simple unencumbered life of a wanderer, influenced by the example of earlier American writers such as Henry David Thoreau and Jack London. In April of 1992 he hitchhiked to Alaska, carrying with him only a bag of rice, a .22-gauge shotgun, and some books. A few months later the young man's corpse was discovered alongside a desperate note in which he begged to be saved. Although McCandless's death was greeted with a mixture of derision and apathy by Alaskans, who pointed to the arrogance inherent in his ill-equipped and untutored attempt to live off the land, Krakauer manages to make his subject sympathetic, according to several reviewers. "The more we learn about him, the more mysterious McCandless becomes, and the more intriguing," wrote Thomas McNamee in the *New York Times Book Review*. Christopher Lehmann-Haupt similarly remarked in his review of *Into the Wild* for the *New York Times* that Krakauer mitigates the reader's desire to condemn McCandless by presenting him through the eyes of those who encountered him. The people Krakauer interviewed emphasize "how particularly intelligent, unusual and just plain likable this young man was," Lehmann-Haupt wrote, the critic also commenting favorably on Krakauer's apt placing of McCandless's quest in the context of other spiritual daredevils and sons of dominating, successful fathers. In this context, Krakauer reveals his own survival of an adolescent trek up Devils Thumb, a treacherous mountain on the Alaska–British Columbia border. Although McNamee complained that the author too readily dismisses the possibility that McCandless's actions were at least partly the result of mental instability, he concluded that while the young man's "life and his death may have been meaningless, absurd, even reprehensible, but by the end of *Into the Wild*, you care for him deeply." Similarly, Lehmann-Haupt maintained that "Krakauer has taken the tale of a kook who went into the woods, and made of it a heart-rending drama of human yearning."

In Krakauer's most well-known work, *Into Thin Air*, he relives a 1996 guided climb up Mount Everest in which he was participating while on assignment for *Outside* magazine. First summited in 1953 by Sir Edmund Hillary, Mount Everest by the mid-1990s had become the site of numerous commercial expedition tours where paid guides would lead amateur climbers able to pay the price. Investigating the safety practices of such ventures, and an experienced climber himself—although not at Everest's 29,028-foot altitude—forty-three-year-old Krakauer joined the small group of men and women and their leaders, two ultra-experienced mountaineers, in their trip up to the summit. From base camp the group stopped at four intermediate camps staged along their route to Everest's highest altitude, each stay designed to allow their bodies to adapt to the depleted air pressure and oxygen levels that gradually weaken and befuddle weary mountaineers. Such conditions attack even experienced climbers; as *Entertainment Weekly* contributor Mark Harris noted, "there is no adjusting: Leave aside the blinding headaches, the gastrointestinal brutalities, the frozen fingers that frigid winds can produce, and the far more deadly possibilities of pulmonary or cerebral edema, and a climber will still face hypoxia, the oxygen deprivation that can reduce his judgment to that of a slow child just when he needs his adult wits most." As Krakauer later realized, it was hypoxia that, when a rogue storm hit Mount Everest, caused those attempting to scale the final, highly exposed region of the mountain to react poorly; when the storm clouds cleared eight people—including the two expedition leaders—were left dead, the author fortunate he was not among them.

"As an inquiry into the outer limits of human strength and into the inner turmoil of survivor's guilt, Krakauer's narrative leaves a reader virtually breathless," noted *Booklist* reviewer Gilbert Taylor. In *Newsweek* Jerry Adler wrote that *Into Thin Air* is "remarkable for its clear-eyed refusal to give the reader even a token reason for ever going above sea level." In addition to refraining from romanticizing the tragedy, Krakauer attempts to place responsibility judiciously, following what Adler described as "the disaster-book convention that the ghastly denouement must be the result of a series of small missteps, each seemingly innocuous." Noting that Krakauer's book "offers readers the emotional immediacy of a survivor's testament as well as the precision, detail, and quest for accuracy of a great piece of journalism," Harris added that, "as the full horror of Krakauer's trip unfolds, it is impossible to finish this book unmoved and impossible to forget for a moment that its author would have given anything not to have written it."

Several years after his Mount Everest experiences Krakauer attempted another daunting project: to unearth the truth behind the headlines regarding a 1984 murder of Brenda Lafferty and her infant daughter at the hands of Brenda's Mormon brother-in-law. "Part *In Cold Blood*, part historical-theological muckraking," in the opinion of *Book* contributor Paul Evans, Krakauer's 2003 work *Under the Banner of Heaven: A Story of Violent Faith* "courts controversy in assessing not only the astonishing success of the Mormon faith . . . but also the history of violence that underscores it." Raised in a heavily Mormon community in Oregon, Krakauer adds to his familiarity of the Church of the Latter-Day Saints by exploring the fundamentalist branch of this religion, a branch officially banned in 1890 due to its advocacy of polygamy. As Jennifer Reese explained in *Entertainment Weekly*, Mormon fundamentalists practice "a harsh, decentralized faith" that has over 30,000 adherents "in scattered pockets throughout the western U.S., Mexico, and Canada." Noting that *Under the Banner of Heaven* "is a departure from Krakauer's . . . macho page-turners about misadventures in the wilderness," Reese maintained that "it is every bit as engrossing." While cautioning that the author attempts to take on too much—mixing in everything from the history of Mormonism to the Elizabeth

Smart kidnaping of 2002—Reese dubbed the book "rambling, unsettling, and impossible to put down." A *Publishers Weekly* reviewer noted in particular Krakauer's efforts, despite his own agnosticism, not to condemn too broadly: while he "poses some striking questions about the close-minded, closed-door policies of the [Mormon] religion," the reviewer wrote, Krakauer also "demonstrates that most nonfundamentalist Mormons are community oriented, industrious and law-abiding."

Krakauer as Both Writer and Mountain Climber

Authors and Artists for Young Adults

Authors and Artists for Young Adults *is a collection of artistic and biographical information about writers, artists, film directors, graphic novelists, and other creative personalities that most interest young adults.*

In the following viewpoint, Authors and Artists for Young Adults *examines the connection between Jon Krakauer's interest in the outdoors, particularly in mountain climbing, and his career as a writer.* Authors and Artists for Young Adults *notes that Krakauer's early writing was all on the topic of mountain climbing and contends that the same interest in risk taking is what prompted Krakauer's interest in the life of Christopher Mc-Candless, which he wrote about in* Into the Wild, *drawing parallels with his own life. Krakauer's own experience mountain climbing prompted his writing about a Mount Everest expedition, according to* Authors and Artists for Young Adults, *eventually leading to the book,* Into Thin Air: A Personal Account of the Mt. Everest Disaster.

"Straddling the top of the world, one foot in Tibet and the other in Nepal, I cleared the ice from my oxygen mask, hunched a shoulder against the wind, and stared absently at the vast sweep of earth below. I understood on some dim, detached level that it was a spectacular sight. I'd been fantasizing about this moment, and the release of emotion that would accompany it, for many months. But now that I was finally here, standing on the summit of Mount Everest, I just couldn't summon the energy to care," writes Jon Krakauer

"Jon Krakauer," *Authors and Artists for Young Adults*, vol. 24. Detroit: Gale, 1998. Copyright © 1998 Cengage Learning.

in his "Into Thin Air" account for *Outside* magazine, later speculating: "Reaching the top of Everest is supposed to trigger a surge of intense elation; against long odds, after all, I had just attained a goal I'd coveted since childhood. But the summit was really only the halfway point. Any impulse I might have felt toward self-congratulation was immediately extinguished by apprehension about the long, dangerous descent that lay ahead."

Krakauer was right to feel apprehension; as he began his descent down Everest a winter storm invaded the mountain top, stranding several of the climbers who had reached the summit after him. Lucky to make it back to camp in the diminished visibility caused by the storm and the darkness of descending dusk, Krakauer stumbled into his tent, thinking the others would be back soon. It wasn't until several hours later that he learned of the life and death struggle taking place farther up the mountain, a struggle that ended with the deaths of eight climbers. Haunted by this tragedy and his role in it, Krakauer first wrote the *Outside* article for which he was sent on the commercially guided Everest expedition. When this format wasn't enough to do the tragic story justice or to bring its author the peace he sought, Krakauer expanded it into the best-selling book *Into Thin Air: A Personal Account of the Mt. Everest Disaster*.

"I guess I don't try to justify climbing, or defend it, because I can't," relates Krakauer in a discussion of *Into Thin Air* with Mark Bryant for *Outside*. "There's no way to defend it," he continues, "even to yourself, once you've been involved in something like this disaster. And yet I've continued to climb. I don't know what that says about me or the sport other than the potential power it has. What makes climbing great for me, strangely enough, is this life and death aspect. It sounds trite to say, I know, but climbing isn't just another game. It isn't just another sport. It's life itself."

Author Jon Krakauer in a park; he survived a mountain climbing trip to Mount Everest when two teams of climbers were assaulted by a fierce storm that killed several of them. He wrote the book Into Thin Air *about the experience.* © John Storey/The LIFE Images Collection/Getty Images.

Mixing Climbing and Writing

Climbing and other risk-taking activities became a part of Krakauer's life at a young age. Born in Brookline, Massachusetts, in 1954, Krakauer was only two when he moved with his family to Corvallis, Oregon, experiencing his first climb a few years later at the age of eight. Krakauer's father, who led his son up Oregon's 10,000-foot South Sister, was acquainted with Willi Unsoeld, a member of the first American expedition to Everest in 1963. Thus Krakauer's heroes became Unsoeld and his fellow climber Tom Hornbein, and his dream became the Everest Summit. "I'd had this secret desire to climb Everest that never left me from the time I was nine and Tom Hornbein and Willi Unsoeld, a friend of my father's, made it in '63," Krakauer admits to Bryant. "They were my childhood heroes, and Everest was always a big deal to me, though I buried the desire until *Outside* called."

Between his early dreams of Everest and his actual ascent of the mountain Krakauer made several other climbs that eventually led to a writing career. It was while attending Hampshire College in Massachusetts during the early 1970s that Krakauer was introduced to Alaska by climbing writer David Roberts. "I became this climbing bum," recalls Krakauer in a *People* interview with William Plummer. "I worked as a carpenter in Boulder, Colo., five months of the year, climbed the rest." Toward the end of the 1970s he met Linda Moore, a student at the University of Colorado at Denver, and married her three years later. Also a climber at one point in her life, Linda believed Krakauer would quit the risky sport, but he found himself unable to do so. As Krakauer explains in an *Outside Online* interview with Jane Bromet, ". . . when we got married I promised I'd quit climbing, and a few years later when I started climbing again I came within a millimeter of wrecking our marriage. So, then we went through a bunch of years where climbing was a big issue. Now it is less of an issue. It is how I make my living, to no small degree. . . . It's a huge part of who I am, and I wouldn't be a writer if it wasn't for climbing and Linda understands that and she accepts it."

Writing and climbing first mixed for Krakauer back in 1974 when he climbed the Alaskan Arrigetch Peaks in the Brooks Range, making three ascents of previously unexplored peaks. These accomplishments prompted the American Alpine Club to request an article for its journal; it was the first article Krakauer ever wrote. Three years later his first income-generating article, on climbing Devils Thumb, was published in the British magazine *Mountain*. With the encouragement and advice of Moore and Roberts (his climbing partner and writing mentor), Krakauer learned the craft of writing query letters and began pursuing the career of a freelance writer; in 1983 he quit his carpentry job and wrote full time.

"I have never received any formal training as a writer," Krakauer admits in an *Outside Online* question-and-answer session. "I have always been a voracious reader, however, and whenever I read something that moves me, I re-read it many times to try and figure out how its author has worked his or her magic. . . . Like any craft, the harder and longer you work at your writing, the more likely you are to get better at it." While trying to hone his new craft, Krakauer wrote several different kinds of articles that drew on his past experiences; since he had been a carpenter he wrote about architecture for *Architectural Digest*, and having been a commercial fisherman he queried *Smithsonian* about penning an article on a commercial fishery in Alaska, which they accepted. "I was setting quotas that I would write ten query letters a week, and I definitely worked hard, but I got lucky," he observes in an online *Bold Type* interview. "Because I wanted to pay the rent, I didn't have any grandiose ambitions of being an artiste; I wanted to pay the . . . bills, so I worked really hard."

As his new career progressed, however, Krakauer found himself focusing on outdoor subjects more than any others. "The problem is that none of them have captured my interest as much as the outdoor pieces," he observes in his *Bold Type* interview. "The pieces I've written for *Outside* magazine are definitely my best work, and they're virtually all about the outdoors." And so Krakauer's first book, *Eiger Dreams: Ventures Among Men and Mountains*, published in 1990, is a collection of several magazine articles originally published in *Outside* and *Smithsonian*. While describing his experiences climbing Mount McKinley, the North Face of the Eiger in Switzerland, and many others, Krakauer attempts to answer the question of why anyone would want to risk his life climbing a mountain. "The reader who knows little about climbing will learn much from *Eiger Dreams*, but Mr. Krakauer has taken the literature of mountains onto a higher ledge," maintains Tim Cahill in the *New York Times Book Review*. "His snow-capped peaks set against limitless blue skies present problems that inspire irrefutable human experiences: fear and triumph, damnation and salvation. There is beauty in his mountains beyond that expressed in conventional sermons. His reverence is earned, and it's entirely genuine."

A Story That Hit Home

The exploration of the impulse that drives risk taking is the major thread that ties all of Krakauer's books together. In 1992 *Outside* magazine asked him to write about the life and death of twenty-four-year-old Christopher McCandless, an honors graduate whose admiration of the writer Leo Tolstoy prompted him to shed all of his worldly possessions and return to nature in search of transcendental experiences. Giving away his savings, McCandless adopted the name Alex Supertramp and wandered through the American West, eventually making his way to Alaska. There he hiked into the wild Alaskan bush near Denali National Park [and Preserve] to live off the land; four months later he was found starved to death.

While researching McCandless's life, Krakauer found similarities in his own youthful adventures, similarities that helped him identify with this young man's life and death. "In 1977, when I was 23—a year younger than McCandless at the time of his death—I hitched a ride to Alaska on a fishing boat and set off alone into the backcountry to attempt an ascent of a malevolent stone digit called the Devils Thumb, a towering prong of vertical rock and avalanching ice, ignoring pleas from friends, family, and utter strangers to come to my senses," writes Krakauer in his *Outside* article "Death of an Innocent." He goes on to point out: "The fact that I survived my Alaskan adventure and McCandless did not survive his was largely a matter of chance; had I died on the Stikine Icecap in 1977 people would have been quick to say of me, as they now say of him, that I had a death wish.... I was stirred by the mystery of death; I couldn't resist stealing up to the edge of doom and peering over the brink. The view into that swirling black vortex terrified me, but I caught sight of something elemental in that shadowy glimpse, some forbidden, fascinating riddle."

Krakauer's fascination with McCandless continued long after the publication of this original article. "I was haunted by the particulars of the boy's starvation and by vague, unsettling parallels between events in his life and those in my own," explains Krakauer in his introduction to *Into the Wild*. And so Krakauer spent the next year tracing the complex and twisting path that led to McCandless's death, the result of which became the author's first full-length book: *Into the Wild*, published in 1996. "In trying to understand McCandless," continues Krakauer in his introduction, "I inevitably came to reflect on other, larger subjects as well: the grip wilderness has on the American imagination, the allure high-risk activities hold for young men of a certain mind, the complicated, highly charged bond that exists between fathers and sons."

Reconstructing McCandless's last two years of life, Krakauer drew from journals and postcards as well as interviews with anyone who knew him during this time period. Thomas McNamee, writing in the *New York Times Book Review*, asserts that as Krakauer "picks through the adventures and sorrows of Chris McCandless's brief life, the story becomes painfully moving. Mr. Krakauer's elegantly constructed narrative takes us from the ghoulish moment of the hunters' discovery back through McCandless's childhood, the gregarious effusions and icy withdrawals that characterized his coming of age, and, in meticulous detail, the two years of restless roaming that led him to Alaska. The more we learn about him, the more mysterious McCandless becomes, and the more intriguing."

"I won't claim to be an impartial biographer," Krakauer states in his introduction to *Into the Wild*. "McCandless' strange tale struck a personal note that made a dispassionate rendering of the tragedy impossible. Through most of the book, I have tried—and largely succeeded, I think—to minimize my authorial presence. But let the reader be warned: I interrupt McCandless' story with fragments of a narrative drawn from my own youth. I do so in hope that my experiences will throw some oblique light on the enigma of Chris McCandless." McNamee maintains that Krakauer does just what he set out to do: "Christopher McCandless's life and his death may have been meaningless, absurd, even reprehensible, but by the end of *Into the Wild*, you care for him deeply."

A Tragic Climbing Expedition

Like *Into the Wild*, Krakauer's next book began as an article requested by *Outside* magazine—an article on the commercialization of Mount Everest climbing expeditions. In order to tell the story, Krakauer became a member of a team guided by Rob Hall, a respected and experienced climber who had been on Everest seven times before. And so one of Krakauer's childhood dreams became a reality. "Secretly, I dreamed of climbing Everest myself one day; for more than a decade it remained a burning ambition," Krakauer confesses in his article "Into Thin Air," adding: "It wasn't until my mid-twenties that I abandoned the dream as a preposterous boyhood fantasy. Soon thereafter I began to look down my nose at the world's tallest mountain. . . . Despite the disdain I'd expressed for Everest over the years, when the call came to join Hall's expedition, I said yes without even hesitating to catch my breath. Boyhood dreams die hard, I discovered, and good sense be damned."

As he became acclimated to the altitude (higher than 17,600 feet) and culture of base camp, Krakauer met several of the other teams and climbers, commenting on them in his *Outside Online* interview with Bromet: "It's really appalling. There's a lot of inexperienced people here—and many people would say I'm one of them—and that's sort of scary. There's a lot of people here who shouldn't be here. And maybe I shouldn't be here. But the guides and the Sherpas make that possible, which is kind of neat in a lot of ways. People who wouldn't have the time and the experience—but they have the money—can do this, so it's neat. But it's a challenge. I don't care how much you paid or what kind of guides or Sherpas you have, it's not going to be easy, I can tell that already. It demands determination and physical reserves. If you can get to the top of Everest, I say more power to you."

By the time summit day was upon him, Krakauer and his teammates had already made three trips (over the course of six weeks) above base camp, going approximately 2,000 feet higher each time. This was Hall's way of acclimating his team to the altitude, a method which he assured them would enable them to climb safely to the 29,028-foot summit. From the beginning, Hall planned May 10th as his team's summit day, mainly because the most favorable weather of the year was likely to fall on or around this date. This, of course, meant that other teams had their sights set on the same day, which could result in a dangerous gridlock on the summit ridge; so Hall and the other leaders held a meeting and assigned summit dates to the various groups. In the end, it was decided that Krakauer's team would share the May 10th date with Scott Fischer's team and all other groups (except the South African team, whose leader declared they would go to the top whenever they pleased) agreed to steer clear of the top of the mountain on this date.

Climbing with oxygen for the first time, Krakauer reached the South Col, the final camp from which his team would make its summit bid at one in the afternoon, several hours before the last stragglers on Fischer's team. By 11:35 p.m. on the night of May 9th, conditions were excellent and the teams left their tents on the South Col and headed toward the summit. The most important thing Hall had ingrained in his team was the predetermined turnaround time of one o'clock in the afternoon on May 10th; no matter how close you were to the summit at this time you were to turn around and head back down. During the ascent various members of both teams suffered from numerous problems, including hypoxia, blindness, and several bottlenecks along the climbing route. Despite these obstacles, on May 10th Krakauer arrived at the summit with two other climbers and began his descent at approximately 1:17 p.m., reaching the South Summit around three. As he continued down from this point, the first clouds began to move in and it began to snow; these weather conditions in combination with the diminishing light made it difficult to determine where the mountain ended and the sky began. The lower Krakauer went, the worse the weather became, but by 5:30 p.m. he was within 200 vertical feet of camp, making it down the final steep bulge of rock-hard ice without a rope and stumbling into his tent about a half hour later. At this point he was unaware that one teammate was already dead and that twenty-three others were in a life-and-death struggle to make it back to camp. The events that unfolded from there made heroes out of some, and are the reason that Krakauer has been unable to overcome his guilt for not having been able to do anything for the other climbers. In the end, a total of eight climbers died, including Krakauer's team leader Hall, and several others were severely injured.

The Impact on Krakauer's Writing

Krakauer writes in "Into Thin Air," "Days later . . . people would ask why, if the weather had begun to deteriorate, had climbers on the upper mountain not heeded the signs? Why did veteran Himalayan guides keep moving upward, leading a gaggle of amateurs . . . into an apparent death trap?

"Nobody can speak for the leaders of the two guided groups involved, for both men are now dead. But I can attest that nothing I saw early on the afternoon of May 10 suggested that a murderous storm was about to bear down on us."

"Climbing mountains will never be a safe, predictable, rule-bound enterprise," muses Krakauer in "Into Thin Air." "It is an activity that idealizes risk-taking; its most celebrated figures have always been those who stuck their necks out the farthest and managed to get away with it. Climbers, as a species, are simply not distinguished by any excess of common sense. And that holds especially true for Everest climbers: When presented with a chance to reach the planet's highest summit, people are surprisingly quick to abandon prudence altogether." As proof of this, one need look no further than May 24th, just a couple weeks following the disaster Krakauer experienced; on this date the South African team launched its summit bid. One of the climbers, Bruce Herrod, fell far behind yet continued alone past the frozen body of Fischer to reach the summit at 5:00 p.m., where he found himself alone, tired, and out of oxygen. At 7:00 p.m. Herrod radioed camp a final time and was never heard from again; he is presumed to be dead, the desperate radio calls and deaths of the previous weeks having had no effect on him during his quest for the summit.

Krakauer's Mount Everest experience has had a deep, long-lasting effect on the writer. Upon his return he wrote his article for *Outside*, "Into Thin Air," discovering only after it was already published that here were some discrepancies in his account of the events that took place. This, in addition to his incredible feelings of guilt, drove Krakauer to turn his story into a book, also titled *Into Thin Air*. "So writing this book became all I could think about; I was obsessing about it," explains Krakauer in his *Bold Type* interview. "Even after the article was done, I was calling people and interviewing them." Once he decided to write the book, Krakauer did so quickly, ignoring those who counseled him not to write it. "I wanted more than anything else to show the complexities and ambiguities of this tragedy," he continues in his *Bold Type* interview. "That it's not simple and it's not easy to assign blame, and it's rooted not in greed and the crassness of thrill-seeking or trophy hunting, but it's much deeper and more profound. The motives for people who climb Everest are, in some ways, noble, as misguided as they often are. It's wanting to reach beyond yourself. There's also a lot of hubris there and selfishness. . . . I just wanted to tell the story in its full complexity."

Writing to Overcome a Climbing Tragedy

The resulting book generated much criticism from friends and families of the victims as well as other climbers who survived the expedition. They accuse Krakauer of being too judgmental of the actions of others and of earning money off the tragedy of others. "In writing the book I tried very hard to recount the events truthfully, in an even-handed, sympathetic manner that did not sensationalize the tragedy or cause undue pain to friends and families of the victims," contends Krakauer in another *Outside Online* discussion. He also answers some of the other criticisms during his interview with Bryant: "Plenty of people have said to me, 'Who are you to assess someone else's role or lack of experience or skill?' But I'm a working journalist, and I was there, and I was there to do a job—to tell what happened as best I could. I certainly feel bad that some people are hurt by my assessments, but somebody needed to step up and tell what went on up there. Jesus, people died—a lot of people died."

Despite criticisms from those involved in the tragedy, *Into Thin Air* was well received by both critics and readers, who kept the book on the best-sellers list for weeks. "Every once in a while a work of nonfiction comes along that's as good as anything a novelist could make up," maintains James M. Clash in *Forbes*. "Krakauer's new book, *Into Thin Air*, fits the bill." Alastair Scott, writing for the *New York Times Book Review*, points out that with *Into Thin Air* Krakauer "has produced a narrative that is both meticulously researched and deftly constructed. Unlike the expedition, his story rushes irresistibly forward. But perhaps Mr. Krakauer's greatest achievement is his evocation of the deadly storm, his ability to re-create its effects with a lucid and terrifying intimacy." *Sports Illustrated* contributor Ron Fimrite similarly praises Krakauer's account: "In this movingly written book, Krakauer describes an experience of such bone-chilling horror as to persuade even the most fanatical alpinists to seek sanctuary at sea level. Not that they're likely to do so."

In this way, Krakauer gets across the all-consuming need for climbers to climb, a need he himself cannot shake even after this tragedy—he continues to climb mountains. "There's something about it that is important to me—for some of us it's an important antidote to modern life," Krakauer states in his interview with Bryant. "But climbing, for me, does have this transcendental quality, this ability to transport you, to enforce humility, to cause you to lose yourself and simply live in the moment. What other people may get from attending midnight mass, I still get from climbing. These are bad clichés, I know, but they're clichés that nevertheless ring true for me." And so through his climbing and writing Krakauer continues to work toward overcoming the tragedy of Everest. "Writing's a way to hang on to your sanity," he concludes in an *Entertainment Weekly* interview with David Hochman. "It's still very painful to me, but I think I've had an incredibly good life and have been lucky in climbing and writing. Now it's just a matter of getting the rest of my life under control again."

The Focus on Extremism in the Works of Krakauer

Gale Contextual Encyclopedia of American Literature

Gale Contextual Encyclopedia of American Literature is a collection of entries covering American authors from many periods and genres, building a broad understanding of the various contexts—from the biographical to the literary to the historical—in which literature can be viewed.

*In the following viewpoint, Gale Contextual Encyclopedia of American Literature discusses the works of Jon Krakauer in biographical, historical, literary, and critical contexts. Gale Contextual Encyclopedia of American Literature claims that three of Krakauer's major works—*Into the Wild, Into Thin Air: A Personal Account of the Mt. Everest Disaster, *and* Under the Banner of Heaven: A Story of Violent Faith—*focus on a theme of extremism: the extremism of wandering off into the wilderness, the extremism of climbing a dangerous mountain in difficult conditions, and the extremism of following the radical beliefs of a religion. Gale Contextual Encyclopedia of American Literature contends that Krakauer's works have been well received by critics.*

Jon Krakauer is an American nonfiction writer, journalist, and mountaineer best known for his works about the outdoors and mountain climbing. His nonfiction works *Into the Wild, Into Thin Air*, and *Under the Banner of Heaven* have been best sellers and received widespread critical attention. Aside from being nominated for a Pulitzer Prize, he has also been the recipient of the Academy Award in Literature from the American Academy of Arts and Letters and Book of the Year by *Time* magazine.

"Krakauer, Jon," pp. 920–923 in *Gale Contextual Encyclopedia of American Literature*, vol. 2. Detroit: Gale, 2009. Copyright © 2009 Cengage Learning.

Works in Biographical and Historical Context

Childhood in the West. Jon Krakauer was born in Brookline, Massachusetts, in 1954 but grew up in Corvallis, Oregon, where his family moved when he was two years old. Though Krakauer himself was not raised as a Mormon, this community in Oregon had a large Mormon population, and Krakauer's experiences with members of the Church of Latter-Day Saints would inform his later work, *Under the Banner of Heaven.* In 2003 Krakauer wrote that "[Latter-Day] Saints were my childhood friends and playmates, my teachers, my athletic coaches. I envied what seemed to be the unfluctuating certainty of the faith professed so enthusiastically by my closest Mormon pals; but I was often baffled by it. I've sought to comprehend the formidable power of such belief ever since."

Mountaineering and Writing. In addition to sustaining a large Mormon population, Corvallis, Oregon, is situated near a mountain range and served as a hub for mountain climbers and outdoor adventurers. Krakauer's father, an active alpinist, introduced his athletic child to the sport of mountain climbing when Krakauer was eight. Krakauer excelled at climbing, a sport that would later take him on the adventures to Alaska and Mount Everest that would inform his books *Into the Wild* and *Into Thin Air.* As a teenager Krakauer was also a competitive tennis player at Corvallis High School, where he graduated in 1972. He then enrolled at Hampshire College in Massachusetts and took up environmental science, which fostered his already pronounced love of nature and outdoor sport. While in college, Krakauer was part of a group of mountaineers who were the first to climb the Arrigetch Peaks in the Arctic National Park of Alaska. For this, he was invited by the *American Alpine Journal* to write about his experience. Krakauer received praise for his article, and began to contemplate a future career that would wed journalism to outdoor sport.

Experiences in Alaska. Krakauer received his bachelor's degree in 1976, and in 1977 he spent three weeks alone in the wilderness of the Stikine Icecap region of Alaska. During this trip to Alaska he met former climber Linda Mariam Moore, whom he ultimately married, in 1980. In 1977 Krakauer published a popular magazine article about a climb he completed, alone, during which he charted a new route to the peak of Devils Thumb in Alaska. After the publication of this article, Krakauer began receiving regular magazine assignments. Aside from writing, he worked as a commercial salmon fisherman and carpenter. In 1983, he abandoned these jobs to be able to write and climb full time. In 1990, Krakauer published his first book, *Eiger Dreams*, a collection of his magazine writing. In 1996, Krakauer utilized his extensive knowledge of the terrain of Alaska to publish *Into the Wild*, for which he researched and recreated the life of Christopher McCandless, a twenty-four-year-old who renounced all material possessions, hitchhiked to Alaska, and attempted to survive in the wild. Determined to live off the land, McCandless carried with him only a shotgun, a bag of rice, and some books. Four months later, his body was found: He had starved to death. Near the body was a desperate note in which he begged to be saved. Krakauer used McCandless's journals and postcards, as well as interviews with those who knew him, to reconstruct the last two years of the boy's life. The book was an instant best seller.

Climbing Mount Everest. In 1996, Krakauer joined fellow mountaineers and embarked on a guided ascent of Mount Everest, arguably his most famous climb. However, their descent from the mountain was hampered by a disastrous ice storm, which left four of his teammates [and four other climbers] dead. He relayed these experiences in an article for *Outside* magazine, for which he received a National Magazine Award. In 1997 he expanded the article into the book *Into Thin Air*. The book was a finalist for the Pulitzer Prize in general nonfiction in 1998. In response to the events he recounted in *Into Thin Air*, Krakauer established the Everest '96 Memorial Fund, which provides humanitarian aid to the peoples of the Himalayan region through royalties from the book as a tribute to those who perished during the expedition. During this period Krakauer also published a *Smithsonian* article about Mount Rainier, a prominent volcano in the state of Washington, which earned him a Walter Sullivan Award for Excellence in Science Journalism.

Examining Extremism in Religion. In 2003, Krakauer shifted away from outdoor adventure and published the book *Under the Banner of Heaven: A Story of Violent Faith*, which explored the history of the Mormon religion in America. While the book discussed the nineteenth-century roots of Mormonism with the revelations of prophet Joseph Smith, it also focused on twentieth-century Mormon fundamentalism. In particular, it focused on the 1984 murder of Brenda Lafferty by her fundamentalist brothers-in-law Ron and Dan Lafferty, and the kidnapping and subsequent brainwashing of fourteen-year-old Elizabeth Smart by Mormon polygamist Brian David Mitchell. Though receiving much critical praise, the book became an item of controversy and garnered much opprobrium [contempt] by members of the Church of Latter-Day Saints. Krakauer's articles continue to appear in such periodicals as *GEO, The Washington Post, National Geographic, Rolling Stone,* and *Architectural Digest.* He is currently an editor-at-large for *Outside* magazine. He lives in Seattle with his wife.

Works in Literary Context

Extremism. All three of Krakauer's major works revolve around the theme of extremism—albeit religious or environmental. In *Into the Wild*, Krakauer chose to chronicle the experiences of Christopher McCandless, a rich, university-educated twenty-four-year-old who decided to give away $25,000 in savings, renounce all material possessions, and seek spiritual transcendence in the wilderness. McCandless eventually succumbed to the harsh weather conditions of Alaska's mountains, for which he was woefully unprepared. Similarly, *Into Thin Air* acquaints readers with the travails of the extreme sport of mountain climbing during the most dangerous season on the world's most difficult climb, Mount Everest. During 1996 fifteen climbers lost their lives trying to reach the summit of the mountain, an event Krakauer would partially blame on unpreparedness resulting from the commercialization of the climb. Nonetheless, the book gives an adventurous rendering of Krakauer's battles against snow, ice, rock, cold, and starvation. In *Under the Banner of Heaven* Krakauer would shift his focus away from extremism relating to the elements, and would explore religious zealotry.

Fundamentalist Religion. In *Under the Banner of Heaven*, Krakauer states that he began writing the book to answer the question "How does a critical mind reconcile scientific and historical truth with religious doctrine? . . . I was fascinated by the paradoxes that reside at the intersection of doubt and faith, and I had a high regard for congenital skeptics . . . who somehow emerged from the fray with their beliefs intact." The result of Krakauer's investigation is a book that explores the faith, history, and politics of both the Church of Latter-Day Saints and their more fundamentalist Mormon counterparts. Utilizing exhaustive research and countless interviews, Krakauer traces the religion's roots in the teachings of evangelist Joseph Smith to its current state in all-Mormon communities in Utah and Arizona. Throughout the book—which focuses on the slaying of Brenda Lafferty and her infant daughter by her fundamentalist brothers-in-law in 1984—Krakauer points out how zealotry often leads to tyranny and violence. In addition, he pays particular attention to how the practice of polygamy can lead to the manipulation or abuse of women and children.

Works in Critical Context

Jon Krakauer has been praised by readers and reviewers for his ability to make nonfiction stories highly accessible and engaging, due to effective structure, narrative skill, and formidable descriptive powers. He is often praised for both the quality and the volume of his research.

Into the Wild. *Into the Wild,* Jon Krakauer's first nonfiction work, was published in 1996 and became an instant success, spending more than two years on the *New York Times* bestsellers list. It tells the tragic story of Christopher McCandless, a recent college graduate who was found dead in the wilderness of Alaska. The book was adapted into a 2007 motion picture directed by Sean Penn. *Into the Wild* was described as "compelling and tragic, hard to put down," in the words of the *San Francisco Chronicle.* The *Los Angeles Times* was also impressed with the book, saying that the story line was "engrossing, with a telling eye for detail," and praised Krakauer for capturing "the sad saga of a stubborn, idealistic young man." The *Washington Post* commended Krakauer for creating a narrative of "arresting force," and warned that "anyone who ever fancied wandering off to face nature on its own harsh terms should give [*Into the Wild*] a look."

Into Thin Air. Krakauer's 1997 book, *Into Thin Air,* a firsthand account of his May 1996 Mount Everest tragedy, also spent time on top of the *New York Times* nonfiction bestsellers list, and was given the Book of the Year award by *Time* magazine. In addition, it was called one of the best books of the year by the *New York Times Book Review* and was one of the finalists for the 1997 National Book Critics [Circle] Award. In 1999 it won the Academy Award in Literature from the American Academy of Arts and Letters. *Into Thin Air* was praised for being "meticulously researched and deftly constructed," according to Alastair Scott, a *New York Times* reviewer. Scott also noted that the book's most interesting quality was Krakauer's depiction of the deadly storm, and commended Krakauer's "ability to re-create its effects with a lucid and terrifying intimacy." In another review, the *Wall Street Journal* simply called the book one of the best adventure works of all time.

Under the Banner of Heaven. In 2003, Krakauer released another best seller, *Under the Banner of Heaven: A Story of Violent Faith*, which investigates the story of Ron and Dan Lafferty, brothers of the Mormon fundamentalist faith who claim that they have the right to kill. The book attempts to uncover and raise questions about the nature of religious belief. *Under the Banner of Heaven*, however, received more mixed opinions than Krakauer's previous books. Many reviewers argued that the book offered a new perspective on the dark side of religion. John Freeman, in the *St. Louis [Post]-Dispatch*, noted that the book successfully exhibits "how extreme sects of the Mormon faith have persisted and continue to operate outside the oversight of the mainstream church and even the U.S. government." Rachel Collins of *Library Journal* said that the book was "a thoroughly engrossing and ultimately startling comment on all fundamentalist ideas." *Book Magazine* agreed by saying that *Under the Banner of Heaven* was a comprehensive study of "faith and violence in Mormonism," and that the book "reminds us of the power of the most pernicious form of evil—evil in the name of God." As expected, however, supporters of the Mormon faith objected to Krakauer's work, citing the inconsistencies in his account of the religion's history and criticizing him for putting the Mormons in a bad light. On June 26, just two weeks before the release of *Under the Banner of Heaven*, church spokesman Mike Otterson issued a statement charging that Krakauer was "promoting old stereotypes" and "tars every Mormon with the same brush."

Into the Wild and Christopher McCandless's Wilderness Adventure

Review of *Into the Wild*

David Stevenson

David Stevenson is the director of the Creative Writing and Literary Arts program at the University of Alaska, Anchorage.

In the following review of Jon Krakauer's Into the Wild, *Stevenson argues that interest in the novel is accomplished by the skillful relating of a true story. Stevenson claims that Krakauer portrays Christopher McCandless in a charitable and even, at times, heroic manner that makes the already interesting story of McCandless's life compelling. He contends that by drawing attention to McCandless's interest in idealistic writers and by adding his own chapter epigraphs, Krakauer places McCandless among the legends of notorious and adventurous youngsters who have wandered the American West.*

In *Into the Wild* Jon Krakauer narrates the story of Chris McCandless, a twenty-four-year-old from the suburbs of Washington, D.C., who walked into the Alaskan wilderness with a small caliber rifle and a ten-pound bag of rice and whose malnourished corpse was found four months later. The first mystery was in identifying the body—a task made difficult by McCandless's deliberate renunciation of the trappings of industrialized suburban America. We all know people who to some degree *choose* the wilderness and make material sacrifices to do so; but not many of those give away $24,000 to charity, abandon their cars, and burn all the cash in their wallets. These details sound crazed out of context, but in Krakauer's view they are the acts of a high-minded idealist.

The larger mystery, and addressing this is Krakauer's real purpose here, is: why did McCandless undertake this strange solitary wilderness adventure that ended in his death?

David Stevenson, "Review of *Into the Wild*," *Western American Literature*, vol. 31, no. 2, Summer 1996, pp. 163–165. Copyright © 1996 by the Western Literature Association. All rights reserved. Reproduced by permission.

Into the Wild belongs to that very small handful of books to receive full-page reviews in both the *New York Times Book Review* and the *American Alpine Journal*. What elicits such a range of interest? Is the story itself so compelling, the writing so polished? Or have wilderness-related tales finally impressed themselves into the nation's consciousness? In this case, all of the above are true.

The structure of Krakauer's tale is not only both thoughtful and thorough, but compelling as well. We begin with the last person to see McCandless alive and move to the discovery of his body. From there Krakauer has reconstructed the previous two years of McCandless's western odyssey, a journey that included a four-hundred-mile canoe trip down the Colorado River from Bullhead City [Arizona] to the Gulf of Mexico. McCandless lived in and traveled through eight western states as well as Mexico and British Columbia before his journey ended.

Krakauer puts McCandless into historical perspective with other western pioneers of disappearance and misjudgment (many of whom were mentally ill), and devotes a full chapter to the precedent set by Everett Ruess, another talented idealistic youth who disappeared, possibly by design, into the desert outside of Escalante, Utah, in 1934. From there the narrative moves back into McCandless's family history, on to Krakauer's own youthful exploits on Devils Thumb on the Stikine Icecap in Alaska, and finally Krakauer's literal retracing of his subject's last adventure—a journey to the outback and the abandoned school bus where McCandless died.

McCandless's critics, and there were many, claimed he was willfully ignorant and woefully underprepared—a "USGS [US Geological Survey] quadrant and a Boy Scout manual" would have saved him. But as Krakauer so sharply illustrates, McCandless was looking for a blank spot on the map in an age in which none exists. His "elegant solution to this dilemma: He simply got rid of the map. In his own mind, if nowhere

Actor Emile Hirsch portrays American hiker Christopher McCandless in the 2007 film Into the Wild. ©

else, the *terra* would thereby remain *incognita.*" We are thus once again reminded that the concept of wilderness is ultimately a construct of the human mind.

In his introspective chapter on his own youthful solo climbing in Alaska, Krakauer makes more explicit his personal connection to McCandless. But there's more to Krakauer's obsession than the mere recognition that "there but by the grace of God go I. . . ." The purity of McCandless's vision and the rigor with which he addressed it (naivete aside) are standards that few even aspire to, much less achieve. Krakauer's respect for McCandless's undertaking the spiritual quest of the pilgrim borders on admiration. In a self-deprecating moment Krakauer observes that in their "intellect and lofty ideals" he and McCandless differ greatly. But the gap may be narrower than Krakauer himself perceives; Krakauer is donating twenty percent of his profits to a scholarship fund in Chris McCandless's name. And he tells the story with more intelligence and heart than anyone has a right to hope for in his or her biographer. If McCandless was not lucky in life (and Krakauer makes a convincing case for this) he is, at least, lucky that a writer of Krakauer's discipline and polish took up his story.

Why should McCandless's story matter so much to the writer? And, by extension, why should it matter to us? In his attempt to answer this, Krakauer begins his chapters with quotes from McCandless's postcards to friends, various graffiti McCandless scrawled at the abandoned bus, passages he'd highlighted in [American writer] Jack London and [American writer Henry David] Thoreau, [Russian writer Leo] Tolstoy and [Russian writer Boris] Pasternak. London was a particular favorite, but as Krakauer observes, "he seemed to forget they were works of fiction, constructions of the imagination. . . ." In short, a portrait of a romantic idealistic youth emerges, but Krakauer is not content to let our memory of McCandless settle into stereotype.

In addition to the chapter epigraphs from McCandless's own hand, Krakauer has expertly added his own choices—from [American writers] Edward Hoagland, Wallace Stegner, Annie Dillard, and [English explorer and writer] Edward Whymper, among many others. One gets the feeling that these would indeed be the choices McCandless would have at some later point made for himself had he been given the chance. Krakauer's selection from Stegner's *The American West as Living Space* is particularly appropriate: "It should not be denied . . . that being footloose has always exhilarated us. It is associated in our minds with escape from history and oppression and law and irksome obligations, with absolute freedom, and the road has always led west."

The American West has always been a place for adventurous souls to reinvent themselves, as McCandless so deliberately did—abandoning even his name and choosing for himself "Alexander Supertramp." In fact, the map of North America printed on the back of the cover with the dotted lines of McCandless's trail looks very familiar. The lines look much like the trail of all westward pioneers from [American explorers] Lewis and Clark, to Alaskan Sourdoughs [experienced miners during the Klondike Gold Rush], to [American writer] Jack Kerouac, to a band of college kids in their parents' station wagons heading west on Route 66 for a last hurrah before surrendering to "the real world"—the one McCandless refused to enter.

McCandless Was Neither Lucky nor Stupid, but Foolish

Suzan Nightingale

Suzan Nightingale was a columnist for the Anchorage Daily News *and commentator for the Alaska Public Radio Network prior to her death in 1996.*

In the following viewpoint, Nightingale claims that the story of Christopher McCandless's eventual demise in the Alaskan wilderness is one of youthful foolishness. Nightingale claims that Jon Krakauer's portrayal of McCandless is unapologetically sympathetic but contends that facts exist about McCandless that set him apart from other potentially admirable wilderness adventurers. Nightingale argues that McCandless created unnecessary adversity and challenges for himself, illustrating that it was his tragic ideology and his foolishness that ultimately led to his demise.

Any Alaskan can tell you about the disaster that got away— the squall that didn't sink her kayak, the turbulence that didn't swamp his bouncing Piper Cub [aircraft], the camping trip that degenerated into a search for the trail back home. These stories usually end in one of two ways: "Boy, were we stupid," or, more likely, "Boy, were we lucky."

The Story of Chris McCandless

Chris McCandless was neither stupid nor lucky when, on April 28, 1992, he walked into the open country north of Mount McKinley. He was young, though, a 24-year-old ascetic who thought that 10 pounds of rice, a .22-caliber Remington and a pack full of paperbacks would last him the summer. He had lived on less.

Four months later, hunters found McCandless' emaciated body 15 miles from the road. His nearby journal read: "Too weak to walk out, have literally become trapped in the wild." What McCandless hadn't anticipated was the summer melt; the shallow river he had forded in April had turned into a frigid, roily tumult that blocked his return in July.

Into the Wild is Jon Krakauer's compelling account of McCandless' two-year odyssey from privileged honors student to ill-fated nomad. With a telling eye for detail, Krakauer has captured the sad saga of a stubborn, idealistic young man who gave away $24,000, abandoned his car in the Arizona desert and eventually even burned the cash in his wallet in his growing disdain for materialism.

Krakauer first covered McCandless and his fate for *Outside* magazine three years ago. That story garnered more mail than any other piece in *Outside*'s history. Many writers lauded McCandless for his courage and ideals; others—including many Alaskans—castigated Krakauer for "romanticizing" the ignorance that cost McCandless his life.

Unique Facts About McCandless

A slew of characters comes to Alaska every year to "live off the land," a term that can mean anything from deserting your family to seeking communion with [American writer] Henry David Thoreau. What sets McCandless' story apart is his own tormented logic, his youthful foolishness and Krakauer's success in bird-dogging the characters who met McCandless along the way. By painstakingly retracing McCandless' steps from the vast Southwestern desert to the wheat fields of South Dakota, Krakauer tracks a young man whose opinions were becoming as hardened as his body. Over and over, drivers who pulled over to give the young hitchhiker a ride ended up feeding him, housing him, even offering him work. Almost everyone tried to give him money or clothes or advice.

In return, McCandless cited Leo Tolstoy, the Russian writer who had abandoned his own life of privilege, as the icon of a life of true renunciation. The margins of McCandless' dog-eared paperbacks were filled with reflections on Tolstoy's and Thoreau's observations, and he repeatedly recommended them to others.

Ironically, as McCandless was cultivating surprisingly deep friendships with people on the road, his family had no idea where he was.

In May 1990, McCandless had graduated with honors from Emory University in Atlanta, bought his mother a Mother's Day box of chocolates—a touching breach of his own self-imposed policy against giving or receiving gifts—and talked of a possible road trip. Walt and Billie McCandless never heard from their son again.

When August rolled around with no news, they went to Atlanta to find that McCandless had moved out of his apartment and disappeared. On returning home to Virginia, the couple were stunned to find all the letters they'd written over the summer; McCandless had apparently ordered the postal service to hold them for return after Aug. 1. A private investigator later determined that McCandless had donated the $24,000 left in his college fund to charity.

A Sympathetic Portrait

Krakauer's ability to engage the McCandless family, and their obvious trust in him, are put to good use. We have not only a "before" picture to offset the "after," we can also glimpse the blurring lines in between. There is an early story of how McCandless, as a sincere high school student, put up a homeless man in his unwitting parents' Airstream [trailer], which was parked right in the driveway.

Krakauer makes no apologies for this sympathetic portrait and in fact weaves a personal narrative of his own troubled relationship with his father into the tale. In two distractingly detailed chapters recalling his own close call while mountain climbing solo in Alaska, Krakauer drives home the point that youthful hubris doesn't necessarily mean a young man has a death wish.

Indeed, as Krakauer points out, there is a time-honored culture of the nomad in this country. It still calls to young men. Alaska is one of the last places big enough and wild enough to draw them—and big enough and wild enough to kill them. In the book, Krakauer also recounts the story of Everett Ruess, a young man who in the 1930s disappeared into the canyon lands of Arizona and New Mexico, where McCandless also spent time. The comparison is an imperfect one, though, because Ruess evinced none of the anger toward his family nor the disapproval of society that festered in McCandless.

As Tolstoy might say, each eccentric is eccentric in his own way. Although Krakauer rightfully reminds us of this odd fraternity, the very detail that makes McCandless' story so riveting bogs down in the book's digressions into other biographies. The engrossing, inexorable tragedy of Chris McCandless beckons.

A Tragic and Foolish Journey

For McCandless, the adversity and challenge were the thing itself. Lord knows, people tried to make his life easier along the way. But McCandless firmly stuck to his course, even as he maintained friendships with many who had given him rides and meals and jobs. One 80-year-old man, whose son had been killed in an auto accident years earlier, even wanted to adopt him.

These people are the true chroniclers of this American tragedy. Using their stories and McCandless' own journals, Krakauer paints a picture of a young man who succeeded in living by his wits and the kindness of strangers for two years before heading for Alaska. Sometimes his fishing pole was his only source of food. When people tried to warn him that summer in the northern wilderness was a different proposition, he was not to be dissuaded. He had trained, he had read, he had dreamed for too long.

McCandless had been in Alaska three days when he finally strode into the tundra, making his way over the April snowpack in cheap leather hiking books and a fake fur parka. He had made no provision for a food drop or a pickup plan—basic precautions for backcountry travel.

No, McCandless wasn't lucky that day he walked out into the country. He was foolish the way a 24-year-old ideologue can be foolish and tragically ignorant of the realities of northern survival. Yet he survived 112 days. Krakauer believes he would have lived to slip back out of the country if not for "one or two seemingly insignificant blunders"—an unforgiving oxymoron where bush survival is concerned.

Given Krakauer's engrossing portrait, one can only wonder what life McCandless would be living today, had he made those 15 miles back to the road.

Adventures of Alexander Supertramp

Thomas McNamee

Thomas McNamee is an essayist and author of The Grizzly Bear, Nature First: Keeping Our Wild Places and Wild Creatures Wild, *and* The Return of the Wolf to Yellowstone.

In the following viewpoint, McNamee writes that despite the many questions that Christopher McCandless's life raises, Jon Krakauer manages to find compassionate answers. McNamee claims that McCandless's desire for a new identity and the desire for seclusion in the wilderness do not easily lead to sympathy. Despite questions of McCandless's sanity and possible death wish, McNamee claims that Krakauer manages to paint a picture of McCandless in Into the Wild *that elicits readers' concern.*

The strangely fascinating hero of Jon Krakauer's strangely fascinating book *Into the Wild* is a young man who starved to death in the Alaskan wilderness in the summer of 1992. That is the starting point of a narrative that seeks to find out why we should care.

An Invented Identity

An electrician who had picked him up four miles out of Fairbanks pressed a pair of rubber boots and two sandwiches on the dangerously underequipped but charming hitchhiker, who would vouchsafe no name but Alex. His parents had named him Christopher McCandless, but in his travels he preferred the invented identity Alexander Supertramp. Alex shouldered his backpack—containing little more than books and rice—and his .22-caliber rifle and walked into the forest, to live off the land or die trying. It was April, still winter in Alaska.

Coming upon the impassable Toklat River, he gave up the idea of walking the 300 miles from Mount McKinley to the Bering Sea, Mr. Krakauer writes, and took up residence in a rusting Fairbanks city bus that had been fitted out as a crude shelter. He then entered on what he called, in a manifesto scrawled on a piece of plywood, "the climactic battle to kill the false being within."

Somehow McCandless grubbed a living from the snows—gathering last year's rose hips and wizened berries, shooting squirrels, ptarmigans, porcupines and finally, in June, with his puny little .22, a moose. He tried to smoke the meat, but his moose quickly spoiled.

By late summer, McCandless's incompetence and overconfidence had caught up with him. The hunters who found his rotting corpse in September also found this note:

> "S O S. I need your help. I am injured, near death and too weak to hike out of here. I am all alone, this is no joke. In the name of God, please remain to save me. I am out collecting berries close by and shall return this evening. Thank you, Chris McCandless. August?"

Dying at the age of 24, he had resumed his real name.

Creating a Wilderness Within

What was with this guy? Why should we care if he had no better sense than this? (The reactions of most Alaskans who read about his death ranged from annoyance to indignation.) And what "false being"? He kept journals, and in between silences would jabber out his "philosophy" for hours, but the Supertramp's ideas are never lucid enough to give us a clue.

And yet, as Mr. Krakauer picks through the adventures and sorrows of Chris McCandless's brief life, the story becomes painfully moving. Mr. Krakauer's elegantly constructed narrative takes us from the ghoulish moment of the hunters' discovery back through McCandless's childhood, the gregarious effusions and icy withdrawals that characterized his coming of age, and, in meticulous detail, the two years of restless roaming that led him to Alaska. The more we learn about him, the more mysterious McCandless becomes, and the more intriguing.

Wherever he went, McCandless sought out the detritus of the society of privilege whose child he was—the son of accomplished, prosperous parents (his father was an outstanding scientist with the National Aeronautics and Space Administration). McCandless detested the world of accomplishment and prosperity. When he graduated from Emory University (with a grade point average not far short of a perfect 4), he gave his inheritance of more than $24,000 to charity and, without a word to anyone, hit the road. What is fantasy in a Tom Waits [an American singer-songwriter] song was McCandless's notion of the good life.

If the world no longer offered the sort of wilderness that freely killed those who braved its dangers, then McCandless would create a wilderness within, discarding the rudimentary protections of modern life—matches, maps, even warm clothing. "In his own mind, if nowhere else, the terra would thereby remain incognita," Mr. Krakauer writes. Hardly eating, never letting his anguished family know where he was, nearly dying of thirst in the Mojave Desert, canoeing a storm-racked Gulf of California, setting fire to the last of his money, he vowed, as he wrote to an acquaintance, "to live this life for some time to come. The freedom and simple beauty of it is just too good to pass up."

The Desire for Seclusion

Mr. Krakauer, a contributing editor at *Outside* magazine, tracks down virtually everyone who knew McCandless in his two

Actor Emile Hirsch portrays American hiker Christopher McCandless in the 2007 film Into the Wild. *The image shows a replica of the bus where McCandless lived and died.* © AF archive/Alamy.

years of wandering. As their memories reconstruct Alexander Supertramp, an image of the young anchorite begins to emerge, so vivid at times that it dazzles, at others so mystifying that one wants to scream. The people who meet him love him, while the reader longs to kick him in the pants. An 81-year-old man whom Mr. Krakauer calls Ronald A. Franz loved McCandless so much he begged to adopt him as a grandson.

"We'll talk about it when I get back from Alaska, Ron," McCandless replied. The author adds: "He had again evaded the impending threat of human intimacy."

After he had slipped away, McCandless wrote Franz an insolent letter admonishing him to live as he, the Supertramp, saw fit: "If you want to get more out of life, Ron, you must lose your inclination for monotonous security and adopt a helter-skelter style of life that will at first appear to you to be crazy."

"Astoundingly," Mr. Krakauer writes, "the 81-year-old man took the brash 24-year-old vagabond's advice to heart. Franz placed his furniture and most of his other possessions in a storage locker, bought a GMC Duravan and . . . sat out in the desert, day after day after day, awaiting his young friend's return."

The Quest for a Compassionate Answer

McCandless's passion was all for the struggle within himself, a half-blind inner seeking for he knew not what—some sort of transcendence through renunciation. The reader never comes to make sense of his spiritual craving, but its very impalpability makes it familiar. Do we not all thirst for something we cannot define? Does McCandless's fanatical determination to find it make him a saint, a holy fool or just plain nuts?

The one weakness of Mr. Krakauer's attempt to understand Chris McCandless lies in an inadequate consideration of psychiatric illness. Indeed, he says straight out, "McCandless wasn't mentally ill." But in a long and engaging aside about his own youthful daring of death, Mr. Krakauer lets us know that he himself has sought out risks that most of us would call insane.

Did McCandless want to die in Alaska? That is Mr. Krakauer's ultimate question, and the whole book can be seen as a quest for a compassionate answer. Mr. Krakauer's anti-hero conforms to no familiar type. His contradictions, in retrospect, do not illumine but rather obscure his character. In death, he passes beyond the reach of mortal comprehension.

Christopher McCandless's life and his death may have been meaningless, absurd, even reprehensible, but by the end of *Into the Wild*, you care for him deeply.

The Lives of Krakauer and McCandless Have Many Parallels

John Marshall

John Marshall was a book critic for the Seattle Post-Intelligencer, *until the newspaper ceased publication in 2009, and is an author.*

In the following viewpoint, Marshall contends that the way Jon Krakauer portrays the life of Christopher McCandless is influenced by certain similarities between the two men. Marshall claims that Krakauer had similar urges and engaged in a wilderness adventure similar to that taken by McCandless when he was about the same age. Marshall contends that Krakauer portrays McCandless as a young adventurer on a spiritual quest, but he is reluctant to draw lessons from McCandless's life and death.

Who hasn't thought of chucking it all, escaping from one's humdrum life and the usual demands, setting out for somewhere else where things will be better, or at least different. Most of us never get beyond entertaining such thoughts as tantalizing daydreams, although some people actually do, to our utter fascination.

A Profile of Chris McCandless

They are seekers, sojourners, visionaries, extremists, people who dance to their own particular music, people like Chris McCandless. A son of the suburbs. A college graduate. A 24-year-old devotee of [Russian writer Leo] Tolstoy and [American writer] Jack London who gave his entire $24,000 bank account to charity and then hit the road across the United States.

McCandless eventually headed north to Alaska, where he walked alone into the wilderness with a 10-pound bag of rice and a .22-caliber rifle and little else and lived by his wits for 112 days before making two crucial mistakes and finally starving to death. One of his last acts would be posing for his own camera, holding up a small sign that said: "I HAVE HAD A HAPPY LIFE AND THANK THE LORD. GOODBYE AND MAY GOD BLESS ALL!"

With these compelling elements, it should not be surprising that a profile of McCandless, written by Seattle writer Jon Krakauer, prompted the largest outpouring of reader mail in the history of *Outside* magazine. Nor should it be surprising that Krakauer's new book, following an additional year of research on the trail of "the enigma of Chris McCandless," is an utterly enthralling read. Krakauer's *Into the Wild* has the pace of a thriller, but the soul of a poem, becoming a haunting meditation on the nature of belief and the allure of the wilderness.

Krakauer, 41, described his young subject's story in an interview as "a tragedy, in the classic sense. Here is a young man who goes into the wild, full of hubris, seeking to do battle with the gods or nature, then suffers bad luck. And what makes it classic is that he knows he is going to die and he faces death bravely, without blaming anyone. He accepts his fate. McCandless' story has all this mythic resonance, of Huck Finn lighting out into the territory, the American romanticism about the frontier, and Oedipal stuff, too."

The Similarities Between McCandless and Krakauer

It is also a story that Krakauer seems born to write. [Growing up] in Corvallis, Ore., the author felt some of the same urges as McCandless did, at about the same age. An absolutely chilling chapter of *Into the Wild* chronicles Krakauer's own youthful quest in Alaska, in which he, "a self-possessed young man inebriated with the unfolding drama of his own life," trekked into the wilderness to complete a solo ice climb of Devils Thumb in the dead of winter. Krakauer barely survived.

"Chris and I are different in profound ways, but one part of us is similar," Krakauer said. "Most people cannot understand why he would leave his map behind when he went into the wilderness, but I do understand the need to really push it, to contrive your own adventure. I'm a climber, and climbers do that all the time—leave rope behind, go after a bigger mountain, limit your tools. Climbers understand that. They understand that the farther out on a limb you crawl, the better it feels when you crawl back."

Understanding some of McCandless' urges did not, however, blind Krakauer to his flaws. One of the great strengths of *Into the Wild* is Krakauer's even-handedness and humanity.

Krakauer's Portrayal of McCandless

McCandless is an easy target to write off as a "kook" or a "wacko," as many readers of *Outside* did. And Krakauer is certainly unsparing in his criticism of McCandless' stubbornness, his foolhardiness, his overconfidence, his cruelty to his own family, which produces this heartbreaking scene: His mother doubling back on the highway whenever she sees a male hitchhiker, in hopes that it might be her wayward son.

But Krakauer's devotion yields a much fuller portrait of McCandless: a gentle soul with a capacity to endure great hardships in the service of his beliefs, as a charismatic person who left indelible marks on a succession of strangers, many from the most humble of backgrounds and circumstances.

"There was something fascinating about him," one relates. "(He) struck me as much older than 24. Everything I said, he'd demand to know more about what I meant, about why I thought this way or that. He was hungry to learn about things.

Unlike most of us, he was the sort of person who insisted on living out his beliefs. . . . I can't get him out of my mind. I keep picturing his face. . . . Considering that I only spent a few hours in (his) company, it amazes me how much I'm bothered by his death."

Krakauer places McCandless' "strange spiritual quest" squarely in the western tradition. The writer includes telling quotes and fascinating parallels from the lives of other western seekers and adventurers, some well-known (John Muir), some more obscure (Everett Ruess).

"I don't explain McCandless," Krakauer said. "I explain by example, offering an impressionistic portrait of this guy and others like him. In a way, I'm an apologist showing we're not crazy, we don't have a death wish, we're just infected with a compulsion to go out there and test ourselves."

Lessons from McCandless' Life and Death

Part of what makes McCandless' death so affecting for so many people is that he was on the verge of abandoning his wilderness retreat and returning to civilization. He had tested himself and found himself equal to the task. He had experienced what he notes in his journal as "the great triumphant joy of living to the fullest extent in which real meaning is found. God, it's great to be alive!"

But McCandless' trek back is halted by a river swollen by snow melt, something he had not anticipated. And he makes a second crucial mistake when he starts eating the seeds of a wild potato plant whose roots had been providing sustenance for him during his stay. The seeds may have been poisonous. Chemical tests paid for by Krakauer show they prevent the body from absorbing nutrients, though the tests still aren't conclusive.

Wasting away, McCandless grows too weak to attempt another escape. After taking a final photograph of himself, he crawls into his sleeping bag and dies 19 days before several other people converge on the site.

Krakauer is hesitant to posit lessons from the life and death of Chris McCandless. That he was trying to return from the wilds, though, indicates that he probably had begun to realize what Krakauer himself has learned with age and maturity.

"Ultimately, the most solo, solitary hermits among us discover that happiness is only real when it is shared," he says. "People are what is important for most of us, our family, our friends. Chris was coming to that realization. But part of his tragedy is that he just couldn't appreciate having a cup of coffee with someone on a sunny day. That wasn't enough for him. But that's what life is, a series of slow and usually unspectacular moments."

Like Jack Kerouac's *On the Road*, Krakauer's *Into the Wild* Taps Primal Instincts

Dick Staub

Dick Staub is a broadcaster, writer, and founder of the Kin-dlings, a movement devoted to rekindling the creative, intellec-tual, and spiritual legacy of Christians in culture.

In the following commentary on the film based on Jon Krakauer's Into the Wild, *Staub claims that Christopher Mc-Candless shares certain similarities with beat generation writer Jack Kerouac. He contends that they both pursued self-actualization in an extreme manner and saw themselves as be-ing on a spiritual quest. Staub argues that this desire to reject the material in favor of the spiritual is a primal human instinct and, like Kerouac, McCandless's story calls upon people to live this examined life.*

On this, the 50th anniversary [2007] of Jack Kerouac's *On the Road*, we see the release of *Into the Wild*, a film based on Jon Krakauer's book that tells the story of Chris McCand-less.

The Beat Writer, Jack Kerouac

Kerouac's riotous "road trip" led to fame as he became the un-disputed voice of the beat generation. Mr. McCandless' 1992 adventure into the Alaskan wilderness yielded less auspicious results—he starved to death only four months into his trip.

Despite the different outcomes, the similarities between the two are striking.

Dick Staub, "Spiritual Searchers Nutty with Independence," *National Catholic Reporter*, vol. 43, no. 42, October 19, 2007, p. 18. Copyright © 2007 Religion News Service. All rights reserved. Reproduced by permission.

Both wanted to be set free from convention and to fully experience life.

At 19, Kerouac described himself as "independent—nutty with independence, in fact." He didn't finish college because he "had his own mind" and wanted to be "an adventurer, a lonesome traveler."

His alter ego Sal Paradise proclaimed in *On the Road* that "the only people who interest me are the mad ones, the ones who are mad to live, mad to talk, mad to be saved ... the ones who never yawn or say a commonplace thing, but burn, burn, burn like the fabulous yellow roman candles exploding like spiders across the stars."

The Life of Chris McCandless

Unlike Kerouac, Chris McCandless graduated from college, but instead of using his $20,000 in college funds to enter graduate school, he followed in the footsteps of his hero, [Russian writer] Leo Tolstoy, and rejected his wealth, donating the balance of his education fund to Oxfam to fight hunger.

Mr. McCandless highlighted these lines from Tolstoy's *Family Happiness*: "I wanted movement and not a calm course of existence. I wanted excitement and danger and a chance to sacrifice myself for my love, I felt myself a superabundance of energy which found no outlet in our quiet life."

In a letter to Ron Franz, an elderly man Mr. McCandless met near the Salton Sea, he wrote that "nothing is more damaging to the adventurous spirit within a man than a secure future. The very basic core of a man's living spirit is his passion for adventure. The joy of his life comes from our encounters with new experiences."

Both Kerouac and Mr. McCandless are controversial figures characterized by immoderation in their pursuit of self-actualization. Kerouac pushed the extremes of excess in city life. Chris McCandless was the extreme ascetic, jettisoning all

Jack Kerouac was an American novelist and author who came into prominence in the 1950s with the publication of The Town and the City *and* On the Road, *a 1957 novel based on his travels across the United States.* © Mondadori Portfolio/Getty Images.

so he could experience the basic, essential human life in nature, unencumbered by the superficial trappings of civilization.

Two Spiritual Seekers

Both were young men who as spiritual seekers were "trying to set their souls free."

That people did not see his as a spiritual quest was one of Kerouac's great frustrations. Ann Charters, a Kerouac biographer, said interviewers "thought he was kidding when he tried to explain that he wasn't 'beat' but a strange solitary crazy Catholic mystic."

To the usual redefinition of beat—"one who is exhausted ecstatically"—Kerouac added the religiously inspired idea of beatific, describing to reporters his search for a more direct, blissful knowledge of God. He compared *On the Road* to John Bunyan's *The Pilgrim's Progress*, seeing both as a search for "an inheritance, incorruptible, undefiled, that fades not away."

Mr. McCandless, who had serious issues with religion, saw his encounters with nature as direct encounters with God. He wrote to Franz, "You are wrong if you think Joy emanates only or principally from human relationships. God has placed it all around us. It is in everything and anything we might experience. We just have to have the courage to turn against our habitual lifestyle and engage in unconventional living."

His final notation written on his deathbed was simply this: "I HAVE HAD A HAPPY LIFE AND THANK THE LORD. GOODBYE AND MAY GOD BLESS ALL."

The Appeal to Primal Instinct

On the Road became an instant success, and Mr. Krakauer's article about Mr. McCandless in *Outside* magazine generated more letters than the magazine has ever received.

Each tapped primal human instincts, the feeling that there must be more to this life than we experience, the belief that underneath the material is a spiritual reality.

I saw *Into the Wild* with my 19-year-old daughter, and I could not help but see that regardless of our age, the restlessness of Jack Kerouac and Chris McCandless taps into our own, calling young people to live an examined life and calling my generation back to a quest many of us left behind when we "grew up" and put away childish things.

McCandless Should Not Be Compared to Thoreau, Tolstoy, and Beat Writers

Bill Gifford

Bill Gifford is the author of Ledyard: In Search of the First American Explorer.

In the following viewpoint, Gifford argues that Jon Krakauer tells the story of Christopher McCandless's life with great generosity. In Gifford's opinion, McCandless possessed a fatal arrogance about his wilderness skills and his knowledge of nature. Gifford contends that McCandless should not be compared to American naturalist Henry David Thoreau, who was not a risk taker. Nor does he believe that McCandless deserves the comparison with American writer Jack Kerouac, as Gifford claims that McCandless lacks the literary and philosophical skills of Kerouac.

"I think I'm going to disappear for awhile," Chris McCandless told his family upon graduating from college in the summer of 1990. Two years later, his emaciated corpse was found inside a bus parked deep in the Alaskan bush.

A Sympathetic Narrative

He'd evidently walked into the hostile outback equipped with K-Mart hiking boots, a .22 rifle and a half-full pack, crocked to the metaphysical gills on Jack Kerouac, [American singer] Jim Morrison and Henry David Thoreau. Intending to live off the land, he had starved to death instead. The last words in his journal were "Beautiful Blueberries."

Bill Gifford, "The End of an Alaskan Odyssey," *Washington Post Book World*, vol. 26, no. 3, January 28, 1996, p. 3. Copyright © 1996 by William Gifford. Reproduced by permission.

Working with precious few clues (and, obviously, no interview), Jon Krakauer pieced together this detailed account of McCandless's troubled, troubling life [in *Into the Wild*]. As he traces McCandless's wanderings around the gristlier regions of American society, from a grain elevator in South Dakota to various countercultural encampments in the Southwest, Krakauer sketches for us a remarkable character. Intelligent, original and talented, McCandless left an indelible impression on nearly everyone he met, but he shunned lasting relationships and treated his family with special cruelty.

The narrative is propelled by two persistent questions: Was Chris McCandless some kind of visionary or a jerk? And did he intend to die? Krakauer clearly empathizes with his subject, even incorporating a long passage on his own McCandless-like journey to the brink, but this baggage, and other assorted literary freight, fails to slow his gripping tale.

A Fatal Arrogance

To escape his imperfect family life and his stifling suburban hometown of Annandale, Va., McCandless gave his $24,000 savings to charity and headed west, where he embarked on a sequence of ever more harrowing solo voyages. Once in Arizona he bought a canoe and attempted to paddle down the Colorado River, only to discover that the river expires in a maze of Mexican irrigation canals. Undaunted, he rode a pickup truck the last few miles and resumed paddling south along the Gulf of California until a freak storm nearly drowned him.

Chris McCandless specialized in getting himself into trouble. Every time he did, some kindly stranger would appear and bail him out, which led him to mistake his good luck for hardiness. So when he finally headed north for what he called his "great Alaskan odyssey," he was frightfully unprepared mentally and physically. Yet he ignored the advice of Alaskans he met on the way (who were quite accustomed to wising up

Actors Hal Holbrook and Emile Hirsch portray Ron Franz and Christopher McCandless, respectively, in the 2007 film Into the Wild. © AF archive/Alamy.

greenhorns) and forged on into the wilderness. "I now walk in the wild," he wrote, insufferably, in his final postcard. The only food in his pack was a 10-pound sack of rice.

But McCandless wanted to be [American explorers] Lewis and Clark, no easy feat in the days of global positioning systems and geological survey maps. There are, Krakauer writes, "no more blank spots on the map—not in Alaska, not anywhere. But Chris, with his own idiosyncratic logic, came up with an elegant solution to this dilemma. He simply got rid of the map. In his own mind, if nowhere else, the *terra* would remain *incognita*."

It was a solution worthy of Thoreau, who conducted his own experiment in solitude just a short walk from Concord [Massachusetts]. It also smacks of fatal arrogance, a lack of respect for nature that would have horrified Thoreau, who was never much of a risk taker. As Krakauer pieces together McCandless's last days, it becomes clear that he wasn't suicidal. Two or three minor and avoidable mistakes were enough to doom the young man.

An Unliterary Character

As hard as Krakauer tries to cram McCandless into a literary bookshelf with Thoreau and Tolstoy and assorted beats, McCandless just doesn't fit. His tale is too rough, too unliterary. His experiences make Jack Kerouac look like a cruise-ship tourist, but he was no writer and certainly no philosopher; his muddleheaded insights are shared by millions of [American novelist] Tom Robbins readers. He was, finally, an adolescent working himself through a phase.

Yet he touched people, most memorably an elderly man identified as Ron Franz, whom McCandless befriended near "the Slabs," a disused military base turned hippie encampment near Salton City, Calif. In a long letter, McCandless persuaded him to adopt an independent, nomadic existence, living off the grid: "If you want to get more out of life," he wrote Franz, "you must lose your inclination for monotonous security and adopt a helter-skelter style of life that will at first appear to you to be crazy. But once you become accustomed to such a life you will see its full meaning and its incredible beauty."

The 81-year-old Franz took McCandless's advice, dumping his possessions in storage and setting up camp in the desert. Day after day, month after month, he waited for his young friend, who would never return. McCandless probably never intended to come back; he walked easily out of people's lives, as he had blithely forsaken his family. Those he left behind confronted a troubling void. "Considering that I only spent a few hours in his company," muses one middle-aged woman who met him, "it amazes me how much I'm bothered by his death."

The Film Version of
Into the Wild Brings
McCandless's Story to Life

David Roberts

David Roberts is a climber, a mountaineer, and the author of On the Ridge Between Life and Death: A Climbing Life Reexamined *and* Finding Everett Ruess: The Life and Unsolved Disappearance of a Legendary Wilderness Explorer.

In the following viewpoint, Roberts discusses the making of the film version of Jon Krakauer's Into the Wild. *Roberts, who is a former teacher and friend of Krakauer, discusses the detective work of Krakauer in developing the story of Christopher Mc-Candless, and he contends that Krakauer developed sympathy for McCandless because of their similar life stories. Roberts claims that director Sean Penn, like Krakauer, takes a sympathetic view of McCandless and developed a relationship with the McCandless family in making the film.*

[C]hristopher] McCandless's story first gained attention as a magazine article by [Jon] Krakauer in January 1993. To expand the piece into a book, the author hit the road, just as his antihero had a few years before. Technically, the most impressive thing about *Into the Wild* is how Krakauer, armed with only the most fugitive clues, was able to retrace nearly every step of McCandless's erratic path as he zigzagged all over the West, driving an old car, hitchhiking, and hopping freight trains, before arrowing north toward Alaska.

Krakauer's Detective Work

Throughout those months of Krakauer's sleuthing in 1993 and 1994, I was afforded a ringside seat. Twenty years earlier, in 1973, "fresh off the turnip truck from small-town Oregon" (as he would later write), Krakauer arrived at Hampshire College in western Massachusetts, where I was teaching literature and mountaineering. He quickly morphed from wide-eyed acolyte into colleague and drinking buddy. Jon was also the only Hampshire student to become my lifelong climbing partner. In 1983, after years of pounding nails to support his climbing-bum habit, Jon decided to try to write for a living.

Ten years later, as he careened around the West sniffing for McCandless's scent, Jon would call me from the road every few days. "Dave, I found the Datsun!" he chortled from an Arizona pay phone. (Three years earlier, McCandless had abandoned the battered used car he'd bought in high school in a forlorn desert ravine called Detrital Wash.) A few weeks later, "I located the 81-year-old guy who wanted to adopt Chris. Chris told him to change his whole life and hit the road, and by God, the old man did!"

For Krakauer, the agony of writing has always crystallized around getting the first paragraph down on paper. By 1993, he'd perfected his avoidance strategy, which was to convince himself he needed to flee the word processor to do more research. Now, as he followed McCandless's ghost, that strategy was paying off in spades. Even while he was burning through his book advance, he was getting to know Chris McCandless from the inside out. Each little find in the Mojave Desert or the South Dakota wheat fields went toward building the character that would burst forth so vividly in the pages of *Into the Wild*.

The McCandless Family

The core question for both the book and the film is, What ultimately made McCandless tick? What drove him not only to his manic escape from society and his solitary death in the wilderness, but to the passionate idealism that fueled it?

For Krakauer a breakthrough in understanding his protagonist came when he won the trust of [McCandless's sister] Carine. Alienated from the family ménage herself, Carine chose to rebel in a more private, less spectacular fashion. Although she remains in regular contact with her parents, she keeps a certain psychic distance. As she told me over the phone, "I went away too. I left. There's just no movie about it."

Months into Krakauer's research, Carine pointed him toward a skeleton in the McCandless closet that seemed to explain her brother's estrangement from his parents. In 1986, after graduation from high school, Chris took off from the family home in Annandale, Virginia, on a cross-country ramble four years before he would leave for good. He eventually made his way to El Segundo, California, where he had lived with his family for the first six years of his life. He knew that his father, an aerospace engineer, had had a first marriage, producing six children. But Chris learned a murkier truth from family friends in El Segundo. Walt had not in fact divorced his first wife until well after Chris was born. In secret, he had kept up the relationship and had fathered another son two years after Billie had given birth to Chris.

In Krakauer's view, Chris came home from that trip with a "smoldering anger" that, after years of brooding upon the deception, would ultimately motivate his headlong flight. And herein lay a deep linkage connecting Krakauer to McCandless.

Jon, as I had long known, had a difficult relationship with his own father. As he writes in *Into the Wild*: "Like McCandless, figures of male authority aroused in me a confusing medley of corked fury and hunger to please."

Sean Penn's film subscribes wholeheartedly to Krakauer's theory, of Chris's emotional wound, which informs some unsettling depictions of his upbringing. In a particularly disquieting scene, Walt (played by William Hurt) screams at and threatens to strike a cowering Billie (Marcia Gay Harden),

Actor Emile Hirsch and director Sean Penn on the set of the 2007 film Into the Wild. ©
Photos 12 / Alamy.

while a preteen Carine, half-hidden by a door frame, watches in frozen terror. In general, Hurt's Walt McCandless is a less than sympathetic figure—until near the end, when the father's grief and sorrow over his lost son begin to redeem him. . . .

The Film Portrayal of McCandless

But does the deceit that framed Chris's childhood really explain this odd, driven, alienated youth? In a perceptive *New York Times* review that appeared when the book first came out, Thomas McNamee wrote of McCandless: "His contradictions, in retrospect, do not illumine but rather obscure his character. In death, he passes beyond the reach of mortal comprehension."

It is possible to find Chris McCandless unattractive and still love the book. Reading Jon's manuscript, I thought McCandless's grandiose condescension toward others was insufferable—especially in the long letter in which he lectures the 81-year-old man he met in southern California about how he's wasting his life. And McCandless's appropriation of snippets from [writers Henry David] Thoreau, [Leo] Tolstoy, and [Boris] Pasternak as mottoes for the true path struck me as predictably callow, the facile idealism of a greenhorn adventurer. But I was completely won over by the book, and not just because Jon is my good friend.

Penn's film sweeps away any doubts about the protagonist. [Actor] Emile Hirsch is simply too good-looking, his Chris McCandless too appealing, for all but the most curmudgeonly to watch askance. In the few episodes Penn invents rather than adapts from the book, he spins rambunctious riffs, such as a rapids-running adventure in the Grand Canyon. In real life, McCandless spent a couple of days in the canyon, but his paddling amounted to a 400-mile flat-water journey by canoe below Lake Mead, from the Hoover Dam to the Sea of Cortez [also known as the Gulf of California]. Penn, however, puts McCandless in a kayak, making an illegal attempt to run Class IV waves, with Grand Canyon rangers in hot pursuit.

For the white-water scene, Penn dared Hirsch to perform his own stunts. Hirsch agreed only on the condition that Penn run the rapids first. "He just wanted to see that the thing was survivable," the director told me. "Neither of us had ever run rapids before. But I was a surfer growing up, so I was comfortable in the water. I made it about three-quarters of the way down when the skirt came up and the water came in, and I got tanked. It was good for Emile to see how quick our safety guy came off the bank and grabbed ahold of me and pulled me away from the fangs."

Adds Hirsch: "As soon as I saw that the rapids didn't completely take Sean down, I was ready to do it. Some people were shocked that I ran them, but no one was more shocked than me. Then I tried it the next day, just for fun, and of course I ate it."

Krakauer's Defense of McCandless

Many of McCandless's Alaska critics point out that if the kid had had a map, he probably wouldn't have died. The USGS [United States Geological Survey] quadrangle of the wilderness into which he ventured clearly indicates a gauging station with a cable across the Teklanika River, only a mile downstream from the spot where McCandless, as he tried to hike out, was turned back by the swollen river. The map also locates three cabins in which he might have found emergency rations and supplies. As I read the manuscript of *Into the Wild*, I voiced the same stricture.

Jon, however, had a compelling rejoinder. McCandless's deliberate choice not to take a map, like his choice to carry only a ten-pound bag of rice into the wilderness, was, Jon argued, the very kind of upping the ante that we admired in other adventurers. Many landmarks in the history of exploration have come about when bold innovators chose not to use all the means their predecessors had counted on. McCandless's deliberate self-limitation, in this view, was like Reinhold Messner climbing Everest without bottled oxygen, or Børge Ousland skiing across Antarctica without air-dropped supplies or pre-laid depots.

A long autobiographical digression in the middle of *Into the Wild* recounts the author's own solo expedition, at age 23, to a formidable Alaska mountain called Devils Thumb. "People told me it was suicidal to try to hike up the Baird Glacier without a partner and a rope," Jon pointed out. On his trek from the seacoast to the base of the mountain, Jon had to negotiate a fiendish icefall riddled with hidden crevasses. His only insurance was the absurd arrangement of a pair of ten-foot curtain rods strapped to his backpack in an X-formation, a contraption be hoped would catch the lips of any crevasse into which he might fall. "I got away with it. Chris didn't. That's the only difference."

Penn's Defense of McCandless

Sean Penn had his own answer to the "Alaska take" on Mc-Candless—the clueless hippie who got what he asked for. "One hundred and thirteen days," Penn says, a terse declaration of McCandless's achievement. "That's more time than 99.9 percent of his critics have ever spent alone, even the Alaskans," Penn elaborated. "It's a long time. It's done a minute, an hour, a day, a week, a month at a time. It's got nothing to do with our judgment of his outdoor skills. It's the strength of the commitment that counts.

"As for those who want to nitpick, I start with the ones who tried to tell the world it wasn't a moose." On June 9, 1992, six weeks into his survival mission, McCandless recorded his greatest triumph in the journal he kept on the last two pages of a guidebook to Alaska plant lore. "MOOSE!" he wrote in capitals, double-underlined. He had shot the beast with his .22-caliber rifle.

The two Alaskan hunters who stumbled upon McCandless's body three months later read his diary, examined the bones of the great animal that still lay strewn about the camp, and declared it a caribou, not a moose. "The kid didn't know what the hell he was doing up here," one of the hunters later told Krakauer, and his buddy chimed in, "That told me right there he wasn't no Alaskan." So Krakauer reported in his magazine article. But the next summer, when he retraced McCandless's route to his fatal camp on foot with Alaska wilderness veteran Roman Dial, they found the same bones. Dial instantly recognized them as those of a moose. Photos later developed from McCandless's camera confirmed the animal's identity. In his book, Krakauer corrected the "caribou" error.

Says Penn, "There's know-it-alls in every section of life."

The McCandless Family's Consent for the Film

If Billie McCandless's nightmare [that she had in 1996 before meeting with Penn to discuss the possibility of a movie] had seemed to shut down all hopes of making the film, what happened to make it possible a decade later? Billie's own explanation is a bit puzzling. "We'd heard that an unauthorized movie might be in the works," she told me over the phone. "So [in that film] Chris could magically survive. And then there'd be a sequel." Billie called up Krakauer and told him she was thinking of changing her mind. Krakauer called Penn to see if he was still interested.

"I got a phone call out of the blue," Penn recounts. "I just kicked up my heels and started writing."

During the past decade, Penn had stayed in touch with the McCandlesses. Of course, he could have made the film without consulting the family. But Krakauer found the cooperation of Chris's parents so essential to the story that he gave 20 percent of his royalties to Walt and Billie, who in turn established a foundation in their son's name. "I always hoped that at some point they would see that it was worthwhile," Penn says. "And maybe this helped: I stayed in touch, but I never talked about the film. I made a vow that I wouldn't push it."

No doubt other factors contributed to Billie's change of heart. Over the years a steady flow of contributions, as well as the Krakauer royalties, funneled into the Christopher Johnson McCandless Memorial Foundation. The money has found its way, via Christian charities, to such far-flung locations as an orphanage in Cambodia. "Basically," says Billie, "we want to reach out to children and help them and their families."

As Krakauer's book attained the status of a classic, it became required reading in many secondary schools and Outward Bound–style programs. Billie says she's received scores of letters from students, and "I answer every one."

The Question of Reconciliation

Finally the long process of grieving seems to have helped dissolve the nightmare. "For years after Chris disappeared," says Walt, "every time we'd go away even for a long weekend, we'd leave a note on the door just in case he showed up."

Near the end of Penn's movie, there is a charged but ambiguous fantasy sequence that portends a reconciliation between the parents and their prodigal son. As he packed up his belongings and started to head out of the wilderness on July 3, 1992, had Chris McCandless finally tamed the furies that had driven him to his perilous pilgrimage? "We always had a strong feeling he'd return," says Walt. "If wishes were fishes," adds Billie.

But Carine says bluntly, "Chris was not on his way back to Annandale."

I ask Penn how the viewer is supposed to read that fantasy sequence—the one scene in the movie about which I had qualms. Is it Chris's fantasy? His parents'? Or a kind of omniscient what might have been?

Penn pauses over the telephone before answering. "When we meet face-to-face, I would be happy to tell you that." Another pause. "It's not that I'm without clarity about what I intended. It's just one of those things you don't want to go on record with."

The Location of the Film

Penn and his producers originally planned to shoot the film in the Uinta Mountains of northern Utah. That choice was partly dictated by budgetary concerns, but, as Penn says, "I'd been to Utah, I'd been in the mountains there, but the one place I'd not yet been as I tracked the story was Alaska. So I called up Jon. 'Jon, is there any way you could shoot it in Utah?'" Penn imitates Krakauer's response—a kind of prolonged intake of his breath. I can see Jon's eyebrows rise, hear his unspoken curse: You gotta be kidding!

"I got it," Penn continues. "So we went to Alaska. I'd never seen anything like it. It was nature on steroids."

Shooting in Alaska meant more than budgetary headaches, however. It injected an urgency into the filming based on the seasons of the far north, as Penn tried to match the changing landscape with the arc of the true story. Recalls Penn, "Either we go now, or we go a year from now. We couldn't go four months from now. The juices were flowing, which is not something to take lightly."

Krakauer was right about Alaska. The panoramas and vistas of the foothills north of Mount McKinley, many shot from the air (Penn: "The imagery just called out for it") lend the film a gravity and magnificence that mirror the quixotic heroism of McCandless's quest.

The Bus

Penn himself visited the derelict school bus in which McCandless had spent his last days—both during filming and again with Krakauer to make a documentary for the Sundance Channel's Iconoclasts series. For the film, Penn's technicians and designers were able to craft two replica buses and plant them near the Alaska village of Cantwell, where much of the footage was shot. The replicas were perfect, says Penn, "down to the rust spots."

Which is altogether fitting, for not long after *Into the Wild* was published, the bus became a shrine, to Krakauer's disbelief. It remains so 11 years later, as hundreds of pilgrims—including some who scorn McCandless as a screwup—annually make their way by snow machine, ATV [all-terrain vehicle], mountain bike, or on foot to the bus. There, they camp out, take pictures, muse upon Chris and his fate, and record their thoughts in makeshift registers that now stretch to multiple volumes. "His monument and tomb are a living truth whose flame will light the 'way of dreams' in others' lives," writes one. "Alex [Supertramp], you have inspired me and changed my life forever. If only more were like you," comments another.

More than a year after McCandless's death, Krakauer choppered in to the bus with McCandless's parents. There Walt and Billie left an emergency first aid kit, with a note imploring visitors to "call your parents as soon as possible," and mounted a brass plaque inside the door that memorializes their son and quotes McCandless's own last message, scrawled on a page torn out of a Louis L'Amour book: I HAVE HAD A GOOD LIFE AND THANK THE LORD. GOODBYE AND MAY GOD BLESS ALL!

Over the 15 years that have passed since McCandless died inside the bus, some of his belongings have been pilfered. But others rest in place—a furry toothbrush laid on a makeshift table, a pair of jeans draped beside the rusting woodstove— like the relics of a medieval saint.

Last June [2007], exhausted by the frenetic pace at which he wrote and filmed *Into the Wild*, tinkering with the last sound mixes and editorial nuances, Penn reflected on the decade during which he thought the project was dead for good. "It really stuck in my head," he said. "I just thought about it for all those years. I found myself talking about it a lot— talking it through and thinking it through. And whenever anybody brought up *Into the Wild* in conversation, I always said, 'That's the one I wanted to do more than any other.'"

The Life of McCandless Was Remarkable and Inspirational

Pete Mason

Pete Mason is a special education teacher specializing in autism spectrum disorders.

In the following viewpoint, Mason contends that Christopher McCandless's life and death sparked unwarranted criticism and were actually quite admirable. Mason claims that although many people would not want to live the life that McCandless did, he contends that McCandless was true to himself and did live the life he wanted. The author argues that McCandless's life has been an inspiration for his own life, prompting the pursuit of self-discovery and exploration.

Jon Krakauer's nonfiction opus *Into the Wild* begins on the cover "In April 1992 a young man from a well-to-do family hitchhiked to Alaska and walked alone into the wilderness north of Mt. McKinley.... He had given $25,000 in savings to charity, abandoned his car and most of his possessions, burned all the cash in his wallet, and invented a new life for himself. Four months later, his decomposed body was found by a moose hunter . . ."

An Addiction to Adventure

While the cover gives away the plot contained within the book, the story behind McCandless' life and how he managed to spend two years traveling around the country as a modern-day vagabond is the story of an American explorer. Even one of McCandless' friends was quoted "[Chris] was born into the wrong century. He was looking for more adventure and freedom than today's society gives people." The thrill of adventure I gained from reading *Into the Wild* and seeing where he traveled is inspirational. Wandering the country for more than two years with no phone, no car, no cigarettes, serves as a lesson that the material goods we all cherish and seek to obtain as status symbols are doing nothing but holding us back from doing what we are truly capable of doing. What is inside each of us—the need to satisfy curiosity, to explore, to converse and think critically, all these are the lessons of Christopher Johnson McCandless, 20 years after his death.

Alexander Supertramp, the name that McCandless went by on his long journey around the country, made his way west from Atlanta, went up and down the West Coast, ventured to South Dakota, Colorado and eventually made it all the way to Fairbanks, Alaska, from which he would set out on the last leg of his extensive journey. In another time, he would be called an explorer, much like founder of the Sierra Club John Muir, who wrote in his book *A Thousand-Mile Walk to the Gulf* of his 1867 walk from Indiana to Florida, all for the purpose of taking the walk. McCandless walked because he was looking for something greater than what he had found in the 20th century, while Muir walked as an explorer in a century when the country was not yet fully discovered. Muir went on to great things because he lived, but had an unknown Muir died after undergoing one of his long journeys, would we know about him as we do McCandless? Likely not, for the ability to trace down information and the whereabouts of Muir would have been impossible in the 19th century, let alone much of the 20th century. But McCandless had his story accurately recreated by Jon Krakauer, then and now an adventurer and writer, who researched the circumstances leading up to his death, tracing him back across the country and over the span of 26 months of travel. Mind you, McCandless walked when he didn't hitch a ride, while Muir walked entirely. Adjusting for time and technology, the journeys are much the same, although Krakauer notes that rather than exploring nature and the world, as Muir did, McCandless did so to "explore the inner country of his own soul." This is a powerful purpose that Krakauer postulates, for in Chris' or your own adventure, you can discover this "inner country" in the way you explore nature in even the smallest of manners.

Said the explorer McCandless, in a letter to his friend Wayne Westerberg, "The joy of life comes from our encounters with new experiences, and hence there is no greater joy than to have an endlessly changing horizon, for each day to have a new and different sun." Chris was looking for something new, on a regular basis, because the new experiences led to happiness, as long as they kept coming. If they cease, so does the benefit of having them. McCandless had an addiction and it was to exploring throughout his life and constantly learning in the process. For all the addictions to have, this was a positive one, and it gives clarity to those of us who still seek to find new landscapes to explore, mountains to hike and places to see. But this was an addiction that ultimately led to his death, forgoing a map in Alaska, not planning in advance to leave the Magic Bus and hike back out from the wild. He was most assuredly planning to return to the world the rest of us inhabited.

An Inspirational Life

Discussions of McCandless' life, either through reading the book, watching the film or hearing passing information about his life, have led to many reactions from friends. I have heard he was a flawed genius, a troubled 20-something, a spoiled brat, a selfish college kid who didn't know how good he had it. I can't say that these all have a little truth to them, because I can't see how he was spoiled, nor do I think that he was selfish, but rather he was an explorer looking for something and once he found it, self-preservation had taken enough of a backseat in his planning that it became the thing that pre-

Actor Emile Hirsch portrays American hiker Christopher McCandless in the 2007 film Into the Wild. © AF archive /Alamy.

vented him from venturing back out to the rest of civilization. What his revelation was seems to have been inspired by [Henry David] Thoreau's *Walden*, writing in his journal, "All true meaning resides in the personal relationship to a phenomenon, what it means to you." With this, Christopher McCandless packed up what he needed and prepared to head out of the wilderness, only to be blocked by the now-raging Teklanika River. Even though McCandless took risks in his journey, he didn't do something that might kill himself like navigate a glacial river. After all, finding his purpose in life after many months and years of self-discovery could not end with the taking of his life.

Although the mistake of trying to be self-sufficient off the unspoiled land of Alaska while searching for some inner meaning to his life may seem far-fetched to some, and not a popular vacation destination for most, he did find what he was looking for in the wild of Alaska, as well as on the rest of his trip. The continuous journey, new each day, provided him something to look forward to with great pleasure each day. When he finally did die, he did so having lasted 118 days in the Alaskan wilderness before expiring. See, this wasn't a short venture into the woods where he was mauled by a bear or drowned in the rapids. Chris survived for almost an entire summer by focusing on survival as he looked for his inner purpose. While some find this in school or in a bar or at a job, McCandless went a long way to find what he needed to live a happy life. The saddest aspect of his life is that he didn't get to live more of his life knowing what was needed for him to be happy, beyond those last days he spent in the bus. But in the least, his journey netted a book that shares his story, warts and all, for others to be inspired by and learn from his mistakes, so that we may see what next step lies ahead for us if we can undergo our own journey of self-discovery.

Remembering his life and death evokes revered pause, for he inspired me to stop wasting life and get off my ass and live. But I learned from his mistakes—to journey with a guide, a map, the thing he lacked in his cross-country quest. This was his flaw and ultimately led to his downfall, but it proved to be the key thing that was needed to live a productive life. Had he lived, it would have been something to know him, provided there was a book written from the viewpoint of his experiences, for he provided the framework for an independent life that was not short on excitement. I imagine him leading an active life, seeking out new quests to undertake and sharing his tales in the process. The latter does not seem to be in his character as we knew him through *Into the Wild*, but for an educated college graduate and traveler who kept a detailed journal in Alaska, it doesn't seem like much of a stretch.

"He was right in saying that the only certain happiness in life is to live for others."—Tolstoy, *Family Happiness*

Krakauer's Theories About McCandless's Death Are Unscientific

Dermot Cole

Dermot Cole is a reporter and columnist based in Fairbanks, Alaska, and the author of North to the Future: The Alaska Story, 1959–2009.

In the following viewpoint, Cole argues that Krakauer has hypothesized three different theories to explain the cause of Christopher McCandless's death, the first two of which have been disproven and the latest of which is not supported by science. Cole claims that all three theories attempt to avoid blaming McCandless's death on starvation and make him appear less reckless and incompetent. Cole contends that before Krakauer puts another possible hypothesis in print, he ought to subject the theory to professional scientists.

Jon Krakauer says that the millions of copies sold of *Into the Wild* during its first decade in print contained what he describes as a "rash intuitive leap" that Christopher McCandless did not die in 1992 from starvation but from eating poisonous seeds.

A Rash Intuitive Leap

That we are still writing and talking about the painful end of the 24-year-old wanderer is tribute to Krakauer's prominent place in the world of outdoor writing and his bizarre quest to invent a cause of death that is not starvation for a man who had almost nothing to eat for weeks.

He wrote in his 1996 book that "preliminary testing" of the seeds of wild potatoes consumed by McCandless showed that the plants contained a toxic compound and that "a compelling case can be made for these seeds having caused McCandless' death."

"If true, it means that McCandless wasn't quite as reckless or as incompetent as he has been made out to be," Krakauer wrote. "He didn't carelessly confuse one species with another. The plant that poisoned him was not known to be toxic— indeed he'd been safely eating its roots for weeks."

Laboratory tests at the University of Alaska Fairbanks [UAF] by organic chemist Thomas Clausen proved that the "rash intuitive leap" was wrong in 1997.

Krakauer must have seen the news reports that year quoting Clausen's conclusion that the seeds were safe to eat, but the book continued to sell and the error remained in every copy printed until 2007.

Just before the movie version of *Into the Wild* reached theaters, the magazine *Men's Journal* published a critical article by Matt Power that mentioned Krakauer's error.

The Mold Theory

In response, Krakauer changed the text about McCandless and the seeds. He came up with a new theory out of thin air.

He said the seeds had been in a plastic bag and that mold had grown on them. The mold was poisonous, Krakauer declared to the likes of Oprah [Winfrey] on TV and Melissa Block on National Public Radio.

"Now I've come to believe after researching from journals of veterinary medicine that what killed him wasn't the seeds themselves, but the fact that they were damp and he stored them in these big Ziploc bags and they had grown moldy. And the mold produces this toxic alkaloid called swainsonine. My theory is essentially the same, but I've refined it somewhat. You know, who cares? But I care and his family cares," Krakauer said in 2007.

Later, a high school student working with Clausen grew mold on seeds to test the theory, but could not come up with a poisonous compound.

Last week [in September 2013] Krakauer formally gave up on the moldy seeds he spoke about with such confidence in 2007.

The Newest Theory

Writing on the *New Yorker* website Sept. 12, he said he agrees with the paper he read on the Internet that claims McCandless consumed a neurotoxin known as ODAP [oxalyl diamino-propionic acid] and succumbed to paralysis, a condition called "lathyrism." The author of the paper is not a scientist, but a writer interested in McCandless. He placed his paper on a website devoted to the book and the movie about McCandless.

"Considering that potentially crippling levels of ODAP are found in wild-potato seeds, and given the symptoms McCandless described and attributed to the wild-potato seeds he ate, there is ample reason to believe that McCandless contracted lathyrism from eating those seeds," Krakauer says.

He said he now has proof that his third theory is correct because he sent some seeds to a "very sophisticated lab in Ann Arbor [Michigan] that had state-of-the-art techniques."

"And sure enough, absolutely, definitely, certainly the wild potato seeds contained ODAP, this deadly neurotoxin that causes paralysis if you eat it when you're not getting enough other nutrients," Krakauer told Audie Cornish of *All Things Considered* in an interview Sept. 13.

When she asked if he was doing this to defend McCandless against the claims that he was reckless, he said yes.

"It was important to me to get the book right, you know? If it hadn't—if the seeds hadn't contained ODAP, I would have put that in a new edition of the book: Well, it seems like the seeds didn't kill him, that he just starved to death out of stupidity. But I don't have to write that now. I can write the opposite."

That would be a rash intuitive leap.

The View of a Scientist

Krakauer claims that his latest theory "appears to close the book on the cause of McCandless' death."

But Krakauer should take the advice of Tom Clausen, the retired organic chemist from UAF who has spent much of his career studying plants in Alaska and their properties.

Clausen said that absent peer-reviewed scientific research he would not make any conclusions about what amounts to a highly technical and complicated scientific question.

The difference between a popular account for a general audience and a peer-reviewed journal is that an editor or two may check the former, while the latter will be subject to critical examination aimed at uncovering sloppy work.

Clausen said he has nothing to refute the conclusion, reached by both the author of the paper and Krakauer, that ODAP was present.

"With that said, let me follow with the comment that I am very skeptical about the entire story," Clausen wrote in an e-mail.

"First, it seems like a rather remarkably lucky shot in the dark for a person to suspect the presence of a specific toxin on so little evidence," he wrote. "Couple this with the observation that ODAP is only reported in certain plants of the genus *Lathyrus* which is not the genus *Hedysarum* and the conclusions are even more remarkable (though not impossible). I would be much more convinced if I was reading the report from a credible peer-reviewed professional journal such as the *Journal of Natural Products* or equivalent. I have often heard a key indicator of bad science that is highly suspect is having its results published in the popular media."

He said that there are two forms of ODAP that are mirror images of each other (known as enantiomers) which would likely have vastly different levels of toxicity.

"Even though Krakauer explicitly states the 'L' form is present in the plant, it is very unlikely that the tests to establish this were done. While this error of Krakauer's is understandable for a non-chemist to make, it certainly reinforces the need for Krakauer's claim that ODAP exists in *Hedysarum alpinum* to be put through a standard review process by technically trained and unbiased individuals," Clausen said.

"Again, I don't make any claims that the report is wrong since I have no data to analyze, but I am skeptical and will remain so until I see a better forum for the results to be published in."

If Krakauer is serious about this foray into the world of chemistry and biology, he should use a small portion of what he has earned from *Into the Wild* to fund independent research that could lead to publishing peer-reviewed papers on whether poison or starvation killed the young man.

If he does this, he will avoid another rash intuitive leap.

There Is Much Misunderstanding About McCandless and *Into the Wild*

Ivan Hodes

Ivan Hodes is a public school teacher in the Aleutian Region School District of Alaska.

In the following viewpoint, Hodes contends that the controversy surrounding Christopher McCandless's death misses an important point. He believes that the extreme opposing views about McCandless—the view that he is a saint to be revered and the view that he is an idiot to be condemned—rely on an interpretation of McCandless as a symbol of something rather than as a normal, flawed human being. Hodes argues that Krakauer's book does not attempt to turn McCandless into an emblem of something and neither should anyone else.

On September 12 [2013], a short article appeared in the *New Yorker* blog, regarding the recent discovery that the seeds of the plant *Hedysarum alpinum* contain an amino acid called oxalyldiaminopropionic acid, or ODAP—a neurotoxin that induces a debilitating paralytic condition called lathyrism. The article provoked lengthy and contentious debate in the *New Yorker*'s comments section and on its Facebook page, was much reported-on by other media outlets, and even drew three grumpy article-length responses in the *Alaska Dispatch* (which themselves were responded to contentiously by the original author). If this seems unusual for an article about biochemistry, it will help to know that its author was Jon Krakauer, and that *H. alpinum* is the Alaska plant that in the

Ivan Hodes, "What Everyone Is Getting Wrong About Chris McCandless," *Alaska Commons*, September 22, 2013. Copyright © 2013 by Ivan Hodes. Reproduced by permission.

late summer of 1992 may (or may not) have poisoned Christopher John McCandless, subject of Krakauer's celebrated book *Into the Wild*.

The Debate About McCandless's Death

The forensic question "Were the seeds poisonous?" is of interest only because it sheds light on broader, more contentious question, expressed bluntly as "How stupid was Chris McCandless?" If, like *Alaska Dispatch* reporters Dermot Cole and Craig Medred, you think McCandless was a clueless, crazy knucklehead, arrogant in his disdain for wild nature and its perils, then you want to think the seeds weren't poisonous; the kid just died of starvation because he was too stupid/crazy/arrogant to make it to safety. But if, like Jon Krakauer (and, in the interest of full disclosure, like me), you have some level of empathy with or sympathy for McCandless, you want to think the seeds were poisonous—he was doing his best to survive a difficult enterprise and was done in because he consumed something that was not known to be poisonous until two decades after his death. Questions of McCandless's motivation, level of competence, and general worth are complicated and subjective, and so subject to probably unsolvable debate. But the debate is most certainly there, which only raises another question: Why do we care?

Millions of people have died before their time since 1992—why does this one particular death continue to excite strong emotion in so many people? The answer is, people don't really care about Chris McCandless, the young man from Virginia who died on the Stampede Trail; they are invested in Chris McCandless as a symbol. The rancor comes because he symbolizes different, conflicting things for different people, and because what we read into McCandless has much to do with the way we perceive Alaska and its future.

The Pro-McCandless Viewpoint

Look at the pro-McCandless comments in the *New Yorker* article. They refer to him as "Chris," as though he were kith or kin, suggesting the strangely intense emotional and spiritual bond some people form with this long-dead man. To readers like this—who tend to be sensitive, melancholy, and maybe even disaffected—McCandless represents freedom, purity of spirit, and rejection of the bourgeois conventionality of modern American life. They see *Into the Wild* as a paean to a Great Soul, someone who was able to rise above the grubby reality of daily existence and achieve a sort of wild sainthood. For the most extreme holders of this view, McCandless's death itself was less tragedy than transcendence, the ultimate exercise in liberating oneself from this petty world. In this reading, the Alaska wild is the place you go to transcend bourgeois society, the church where you achieve sainthood. It follows from this worldview that the sacred Wild must be preserved and protected from tawdry and shallow enterprises like development and resource extraction.

The Anti-McCandless Viewpoint

Now, read through the anti-McCandless comments and note the severity and mean-spiritedness of tone. Those prone to dislike him suggest he got exactly what he deserved, as though making mistakes while living in backcountry Alaska as a 23-year-old renders someone forever unworthy of the most basic human sympathy. The tone is always of the Wise Sourdough, the pragmatic, commonsense Alaskans (and it is mostly Alaskans) who Just Know Better, like the old men in Jack London stories. For readers like this, deriding McCandless is a way of nourishing their own sense of self-regard: *If McCandless is stupid and incompetent then I am smart and competent; I have lived in Alaska for many years and perhaps traversed its backcountry, and I am not dead; I have survived the Darwinian struggle and have been deemed fit to survive.* This is attributed to having "real respect" for nature, which means not mystifying and venerating it.

McCandless, at least to readers like these, symbolizes fuzzy-headed, tree-hugging liberalism of the sort that wants to cavort in—and preserve from development—Wild Nature. It's the attitude that's right now trying to shut down Pebble Mine [a mineral exploration project] and keep "locked up" the millions of acres protected by the Alaska National Interest Lands Conservation Act; the attitude of dumb-ass Outsiders who don't really understand the Way It Really Is. The cult of personality that has accrued around McCandless must be frustrating for Alaskans like these: the more people buy into it, the more the "Alaskan way of life" comes under threat from hippies and environmentalists.

People Are Not Symbols

Both of these understandings of McCandless-as-emblem are missing an important point and, perhaps, misunderstanding the book. The important point: *Into the Wild* is not actually a book about Chris McCandless—it's a book about one complicated, interesting, troubled guy (Jon Krakauer) trying to understand and process the early death of another. Krakauer is constantly injecting his own thoughts and ideas into the narrative—most tellingly, the long narration of his own nearly-fatal ascent of the Stikine Ice Cap in southeast Alaska. In certain points, there is a hint of desperation about his inquiry: Krakauer doesn't just want to know, he *needs* to know what happened, because he looked into the dead face of McCandless and saw his own. He felt empathy, and needed to understand the circumstances—psychological and physical—that caused McCandless to die and himself to live and grow gray.

Seen this way, McCandless is not an emblem of anything, and that's the way it should be—because in the real world, people aren't symbols. McCandless was not a transcendent saint, nor was he a bumbling, arrogant disrespecter of nature, and to press him into service as an emblem of anything is a mistake. If we examine the life of another and don't see them as a fellow person—if we don't look into a dead face and see our own—we're missing something important. Christopher McCandless was deeply kind and supremely selfish; tremendously brave and jaw-droppingly foolish; impressively competent and staggeringly inept; that is to say, he was hewn from the same crooked timber as the rest of us.

Social Issues
in Literature

CHAPTER 3

Contemporary Perspectives on the Wilderness Adventure

The Wilderness Adventure Offers a Path to Self-Actualization

Stacy Taniguchi

Stacy Taniguchi is an associate professor of recreation management at the Marriott School of Management at Brigham Young University.

In the following viewpoint, Taniguchi argues that a wilderness adventure can help teach individuals valuable lessons on the path to self-actualization. Taniguchi contends that experiences in nature are less about doing things in or to nature and more about changing the self. He recounts three wilderness adventures in support of his view that extreme experiences in nature facilitate deep and meaningful change in human beings.

Abraham Maslow [American psychologist] probably didn't have wilderness adventures in mind when developing his model of self-actualization in 1943. But the influential psychologist, who built upon the earlier work of psychiatrist Kurt Goldstein, surely would agree that confronting whales only a few feet away, backpacking through drenched and secluded ridges, and treading around icy crevasses apply to his schematic. Maslow argued that individuals striving for self-actualization, the ultimate level in his "hierarchy of needs," must rely on "the full use and exploitation of talents, capacities, potentialities, etc." People who test themselves in nature are compelled to do so too. Indeed, as a wilderness guide and instructor for 25 years, I've helped others realize their dreams

Stacy Taniguchi, "The Nature of Knowledge: What I've Learned from the Great Outdoors," *Phi Kappa Phi Forum*, vol. 93, no. 2, Summer 2013, pp. 14–17. Copyright © by Stacy Taniguchi. By permission of the publishers.

and discover their capabilities while maximizing my own proficiencies and understanding myself better. Nature teaches us invaluable lessons.

The Self in the Wilderness

Wilderness enthusiasts often talk of such things. Sir Edmund Hillary, the New Zealand beekeeper who in 1953 became the first person to summit Mount Everest, stated, "It's not the mountain we conquer, but ourselves." The grueling journey proved more revealing for the 33-year-old than the ascent itself to the top of the world's highest mountain at 29,035 feet above sea level. In 2003, Aron Ralston, a 27-year-old solo adventurist, spent more than 100 hours trapped in a remote Utah canyon after his right arm got pinned beneath a boulder he had dislodged on a rappel. Ralston eventually concluded that his only option was to sever the limb, sawing it off with a dull pocketknife. He said the ordeal "has affirmed my belief that our purpose as spiritual beings is to follow our bliss, seek our passions, and live our lives as inspirations to each other." For him that meant contributing to others, especially his son, a vision of whose impending birth inspired Ralston to risk excruciating pain and bleeding out to extradite himself from being stuck between a rock and a hard place. Jan Reynolds, the first and only woman to circumnavigate the Everest massif, finished her 300-mile odyssey in 1981 in four months with partner Ned Gillette. Afterward, she opted for a warm bath in Lhasa, Tibet, to celebrate. While soaking, the 26-year-old reflected, "The bad food, the cold, the strain, the hard work, and the danger were nothing compared to what I had learned, felt, and shared with people who were more to me than friends. I supposed this was my own answer to why I did it." British explorer Ernest Shackleton undertook a failed effort in 1914 to be the first to cross Antarctica. After his ship called *Endurance* became trapped in ice, he and the crew of 27 braved 17 months of bitter weather, little food, much sickness, ocean

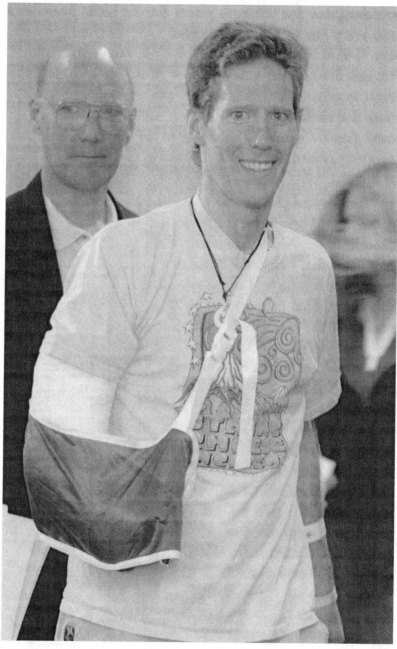

Mountain climber Aron Ralston arrives at his first public appearance at St. Mary's Hospital, May 8, 2003, in Grand Junction, Colorado. Ralston survived a climbing accident that forced him to cut off his arm below the elbow after being pinned for five days. Larry Ralston, Aron's father, follows behind. © Reuters/Corbis.

crossings, and floe breakups before coming home safely, each and every one of them. Shackleton later observed, "We had seen God in His splendors, heard the text that Nature renders. We had reached the naked soul of man." He and his mates came to grips with themselves and bonded, with each other in ways few could fathom—to such a degree that many of the crew planned another expedition to the Antarctic, this time on a ship named *Quest*. (But Shackleton died en route in 1922 at age 47.)

The German philosopher Immanuel Kant intuited that the natural world brings out the naked soul of humanity. I'd echo Shackleton by adding particularly when facing extremes. Kant postulated that knowledge transcends experience and requires comprehension beyond the empirical senses. Kant referred to this as analytical judgment. If he sat by himself on a hill, appreciating the pastoral splendor, Kant analogized, no matter how well he subsequently recounted the episode to others, they would not be able to understand fully the rapture he had taken in. You had to be there. Kant called this sensing the sublime nature found in all things, even in us humans. But, it seems to me, we often don't perceive our own sublime nature because of the layers we adorn ourselves with. The reasons are many, including family responsibilities, daily obligations, societal expectations, educational steps, career goals, and personal aspirations. To obtain the self-actualization Maslow refers to, and these famous adventurers reference, such strata need to be removed. And one mechanism to make this happen is the wilderness, challenging oneself in it.

Put another way, Walter Bonatti, an Italian mountaineer who pioneered many difficult climbing routes in Europe and the Himalayas in the 1950s and '60s, declared, "Mountains are the means, the man [i.e., human being] is the end. The goal is not to reach the tops of mountains, but to improve the man." I second this tenet. Helping my clients actualize their dreams allows me to tap into my own sublime nature. I see people disclose their pure self in the wilderness, where they're shorn of facades that hide and impede. The grandeur of the outdoors inspires them—and its jeopardy obliges them—to find their place among nature's other inhabitants, and we have shared in the mutual uplift inherent in such opportunities. Many of my clients feel grateful to be alive because of these endeavors, and for me, that's Maslow's transcendent level. What follows are some of their stories, and mine.

A Whale of a Story

A novice wilderness adventurer wanting to "live life to the fullest," as she phrased it, booked a weeklong kayaking trip with me off the Kenai Peninsula of Alaska in summer 1992. Sea kayaking, requiring only minimal skills at paddling, offers beginners an interactive close-up of nature. This young stockbroker from San Francisco, plus five additional clients, looked forward to contemplating calving glaciers the size of the Empire State Building and spotting sea creatures such as whales, seals and puffins, while leisurely traversing deep fjords and protected coves. She got what she came for—and then some!

One morning our septet wended over to a creek with hundreds of coho salmon. These silver-colored beauties, which migrate upstream to their birthplace to spawn once and eventually die, average 8 pounds and make for easy fishing and delicious eating. I demonstrated how best to catch them from the banks, and within minutes, we reeled in our limit for dinner, releasing the rest to honor the cycle of nature. "There is certainly something in angling," remarked the 19th-century American writer Washington Irving in his tale "The Angler," "that tends to produce a gentleness of spirit and a pure serenity of mind." The rhythm of our activity, set against the pristine backdrop of cascading waterfalls amid thick spruce trees, indeed put us in a mellow trance.

We skimmed the ocean calm back toward camp, talking of the beauty of the surroundings and the satisfactions of the outing. I intended to expand on these sentiments but noticed a swirl of water roughly 100 yards from the double kayak the stockbroker and I shared as the lead vessel. I thought the disturbance was a school of salmon transitioning to freshwater. As I was about to alert the group to this photo opportunity, a humpback whale's fluke (tailfin) shot up from beneath the surface.

Based on its size and trajectory, I calculated that the leviathan hovered too close for comfort. Such a behemoth could easily capsize our kayak by breaching or simply slapping its fluke on the frigid water, and within minutes the stockbroker and I would die of hypothermia. Trying to remain calm, and saying nothing of the menace, I peered into the greenish blue off the starboard side, searching for the whale's body. The stockbroker, excited at her personal reckoning, remained oblivious to the mortal threat, as did the others, who also were susceptible to swamping, even at then separation from us.

After some focusing, I confirmed the worst: The humpback was only inches below the surface and heading broadside to our kayak. Its fluke still loomed in the air. I feared it would hammer down at any moment.

A Sublime Moment

What happened next was one of those incredible moments Kant refers to as sublime. The humpback, some 30 feet long, gently lowered its fluke into the water without so much as a ripple and slowly glided under our boat and away from the others. The whale was close enough that the stockbroker and I could see the barnacles on its back and could have reached over the gunwale to touch it. We screamed in disbelief, awe, and delight. The others were just as stunned from their distance, wishing they had taken out their cameras.

Our kayak rocked lightly in the current caused by the whale, which suddenly dove into the deep. We never saw it again.

"Sometimes we are lucky enough to know that our lives have been changed," noted oceanographer Jacques Cousteau, "to discard the old, embrace the new, and run headlong down an immutable course." That humpback provided us with such a moment—the realization that pursuing the thrill of life can dovetail with the risk of death, especially in the primitive world—and we talked about the experience for the rest of the trip. And beyond.

Weathering the Storm

"Man must be made conscious of his origin as a child of Nature," wrote John Muir, a naturalist and explorer who advocated for the establishment of U.S. national parks and co-founded the Sierra Club grassroots environmental organization in 1892 and served as its first president. "Brought into right relationship with the wilderness he would see that he was not a separate entity endowed with a divine right to subdue his fellow creatures and destroy the common heritage, but rather an integral part of a harmonious whole."

In the outdoors, sometimes this awareness occurs under duress—a dream becoming a nightmare—as a retired CIA [Central Intelligence Agency] worker and I apprehended on a 10-day hike in summer 1993. Backpacking in the northern foothills of the Wrangell Mountains in the 13.2 million-acre Wrangell–St. Elias National Park of eastern Alaska, this senior adventurer and I relied on the full use and exploitation of our talents, capacities and potentialities, to borrow from Maslow, to survive a torrential rainstorm.

This expanse contained no man-made trails, only paw paths of Dall sheep and caribou, and no bridges, only intermittent shallows in swift creeks to wade. Thus, as Muir urged, we had to integrate ourselves with the primeval surroundings.

Indeed, without signs telling us where to turn or how much farther to a campsite, we went back to basics: maps and a compass. We had taken no chances with other supplies either, cramming our backpacks with freeze-dried meals, water purifiers, mosquito repellant, changes of clothes, and a first-aid kit. I also carried a loaded shotgun and extra ammunition.

Cold rain pounded nonstop the first four days. The showers pelted our tent, so sleep was hard to come by. Flash floods streaked the mountainside, unearthing rocky ditches to trudge. Cresting rivers and creeks meant taking circuitous routes to keep our general course. Everything—deluged land, soggy brush, soaked animals—seemed overcome with waterlogged weariness.

Our spirits lifted the next evening when the teeming let up, and the midnight sun cast a golden glow. Because of the havoc the rains had wreaked on the terrain, I determined that we should make camp on a creek's higher bench instead of lower sandbars, as gravity causes the force of destruction downward. After savoring our first meal outside the tent and trying to dry out, we decided to retire early to our sleeping bags since we had a long haul the next morning. Before turning in, we made room in our backpacks for all remaining food and the other odorous items, and since there was no tree in the vicinity on which to hang them in case the smells lured a prowling bear, I stashed the gear on a ledge at the most distant yet still accessible point from our tent. The lullaby of the gurgling brook helped us sleep easy.

But around 3 a.m. we awoke to the roar of a gushing river and the rumble of descending boulders as the downpour resumed. I poked my head out of our tent. The gentle rivulet had become a coursing current mere inches away and rocks the size of cars, pried into motion by the inundation, were rolling by us as if in morning commute.

Dealing Solely with Survival

We needed to move to even higher ground immediately, but I couldn't eye our backpacks. Without them, all we had were the clothes on our backs and a few basics used the night before like a knife and the sleeping bags, plus my shotgun, which always stayed with me. Instructing my client to pack up our tent, and forgoing socks and shoes since every second counted, I ransacked the sodden campsite and then the adjacent riverbank. Not locating our stockpile, I dashed downstream about one-half mile in case the backpacks had gotten hung up in the shore's brush, but no such luck. Instantly, we dropped from what Maslow considered the highest level of needs—self-actualization—to the lowest—physiological!

Returning to our campsite, I cut the tent's guy lines to jerry-rig a carryall for the scant things we still had on us. The early morning skies cleared, offering some small consolation, and we set afoot, navigating by my memory since I had been through this area many times. We hiked for about six hours down the saturated valley, eating blueberries from bushes, until arriving at a familiar mountain gully. I knew it led to a pass that opened to another valley that connected to a lake that would be our pickup point five days away.

Tired, hungry, and thirsty, we began climbing the gully. I kept glancing over my shoulder; soon we would put the flooded creek and our missing backpacks behind us. I cast one last look. At first, all I saw were creek braids. Then I noticed a stand of cottonwood trees on a gravel bar in the middle of the creek bed. Each tree sported innumerable green leaves. Except a smaller cluster in one had begun to yellow, probably because of the early autumn-like temperatures, I guessed—until it dawned on me that my backpack was yellow.

Telling my client I had to check this out, I ran down the gully, stripped to my underwear, and waded through waist-high freezing waters to get to the trees. And, sure enough, my backpack teetered on a branch. I climbed about 20 feet to retrieve it. Though mangled, the backpack still protected all of the contents, from food to equipment. While we never found the other pack, we could make do with these essentials. No longer subdued by grim survival brought on by the elements, we were again part of Muir's harmonious whole of nature.

The Apex of Soul-Searching

The risks of climbing towering mountains encompass more than slamming into skin-piercing and bone-breaking stone, falling to a certain death, or developing high altitude sickness, frostbite or hypothermia. Glaciers create another hazard. These huge masses of ice flow slowly downhill just like a river, but the lack of uniform fluidity causes some sections to move at a different pace than others, thus forming cracks, or crevasses. Plunging into one of these frozen pits often means injuries and may spell doom.

Especially at Mount McKinley, North America's highest summit at 20,320 feet above sea level. Because the mountain (also called Denali by Alaskan natives) is at a latitude only three degrees shy of the Arctic Circle, snow and ice prevail. Thus, glaciers surround McKinley's base and measure up to 3,000 feet thick. The result: enormous crevasses. Some of these fissures are so big they can swallow a bus without it touching the sidewalls or anyone hearing it crash at the bottom. So when traversing these icy floors, avoiding crevasses is job one. This is relatively easy to do when the splits are visible but nerve-racking when snow cover renders them invisible and each step needs to be analyzed. Precautions including being roped up with partners are essential.

In summer 1994, a client and I faced imminent death after stumbling into one of these chasms. How did we escape? Partly from the full use and exploitation of the talents, capacities, and potentialities of myself and other experts, to paraphrase Maslow, and partly from the spiritual being, as Ralston terms it, in me.

The climb itself was onerous because we had to turn back seven days into the three-week itinerary when the client, a middle-aged police officer from Anchorage and a West Point graduate, succumbed to the altitude at about 15,000 feet. He reported headaches and suffered nausea, despite being supremely fit. When he began to spit up blood, we decided the best thing was to abandon his dream of mastering this legendary peak and get him home in time to recuperate for another dream: his wedding in a few weeks. (My co-guide continued up the mountain with the other eight group members.)

The final segment of our descent comprised six miles of glaciers riven with crevasses. A straight line would have taken us less than two hours, but the rifts forced us to zigzag, tripling the time. Unseasonably warm temperatures softened the snow, so I postholed (sunk to my knees) almost every step and occasionally trod onto a rickety snow bridge spanning a perilous crevasse. Complicating matters, a dense fog blended the contours of the glacier together and blinded our points of reference, so I led the way by compass. For safety, my client and I were tied together by a rope 50 feet apart.

Four hours into maneuvering through this chilling minefield, I felt the foundation beneath me give way and I plopped through to my armpits. My feet dangled over a gaping crevasse I couldn't see the bottom of and my arms clutched the precarious snow bridge I had tripped over. Painstakingly, I removed my pack and pushed myself out. I pointed to the hole and cautioned my client not to follow my tracks but to skirt left or right. He motioned acknowledgement.

A Fateful Moment

I turned ahead and continued onward, methodically checking the firmness of the snow in front of me with my ski poles before stepping. After a few minutes of this agonizing process, I felt a jerk on my waist and was flat on my back, sliding in reverse towards the crevasse that my client, despite taking heed,

117

had tumbled into. In seconds I would follow him, hurtling into the ice chest of a crypt; unless I could halt the terrible momentum of his freefall, we'd both be goners.

I knew I had to grab my ice axe and stick it hard into the glacial plane. But the axe was on my backpack. Which side? The wrong reach would seal our fate. I always choose the locked half of double doors and never inspect the viable places when first searching for my keys, so the odds were not good. But with the fatal abyss fast approaching, somehow I guessed correctly, pulled the axe from my pack, and slammed the tool into the unforgiving turf, halting with a yank with less than 10 feet to spare.

I was saved, but although my client would not plummet to his death, he now swayed 40 feet inside the cavity at the other end of the rope. In minutes I strengthened the anchor my ice axe had become by pounding in snow stakes on attaching lines and by reinforcing all driven points with small weights from my backpack. I then freed myself from the taut rope and crawled over to the crevasse. My client said he was OK. But if I didn't get him out soon, he would freeze to death in the glacial icebox.

I called for help on my CB radio, but no one answered. My client quickly grew hypothermic. I melted ice and boiled water, poured it into my thermos, and lowered the bottle down to him to drink to try to keep his core body temperature warm. But four hours later, he was perishing. His speech slurred and he wanted to go to sleep. I kept reminding him of his impending wedding, but to no avail, and he seemed to nod off every few minutes. With still no answer on the radio, I was desperate.

So I prayed.

I tried the radio one more time. A reply! A mountain ranger, in the vicinity on a scouting assignment, had just woken up and heard my mayday. He called a rescue helicopter via satellite phone and skied down from his camp about 25 minutes away. Within two hours, we extricated my client from his subzero tomb, insulated him in a sleeping bag surrounded by hot water bottles, and had him en route to a hospital. His core body temperature was 94 degrees Fahrenheit, medical personnel said, one degree below the onset of hypothermia. But he made a full recovery, in time for the wedding, which, I'm happy to say, I attended.

Some might contend that God had nothing to do with saving my client's life. But this miracle epitomized Kant's sublime nature for me. Or, as Shackleton put it, I had seen God in His splendors and heard the text that Nature renders. I had reached the naked soul of man.

The Motivation for Dreams

I think the motivation for many of our dreams stems from a desire for self-actualization. I think there's no better way to get there than by baring the sublime nature in each of us. I think the wilderness can be a conduit for all this because it elicits our strengths and weaknesses, joys and fears, while confirming and upending expectations. I think it's inevitable—and essential—that we turn our time in the outdoors into stories to give definition to our existence, particularly if the adventures involve the possibility of death, since doing so facilitates our sublime nature and self-actualization. I think I lead people into the hinterlands for epiphanies to find out who I really am.

"Life should not be a journey to the grave with the intention of arriving safely in a pretty and well preserved body," opined gonzo journalist Hunter S. Thompson, "but rather to skid in broadside in a cloud of smoke, thoroughly used up, totally worn out, and loudly proclaiming 'Wow! What a Ride!'"

Exactly.

The Reaction to Young, Solitary Wilderness Explorers Splits Along Gender Lines

Kate Tuttle

Kate Tuttle writes "In Brief," a weekly book review column for the Boston Globe.

In the following viewpoint, Tuttle contends that the recent resurgence of interest in a young wilderness explorer who vanished, Everett Ruess, illustrates that the interest in and admiration for the solitary wilderness adventure is more common among men than among women. Tuttle argues that there is a history of seeing the solitary adventure as a marker of manhood, such as with writer Henry David Thoreau, but she finds the solitary wilderness pursuits of people like Ruess and Thoreau less than admirable.

In 1930 Everett Ruess left his Los Angeles home and began a series of solitary wanderings through the Southwest. Just 16 and still in high school, accompanied mostly by burros, once by horses, and briefly by a dog he named Curly, Everett hiked throughout the mesas and canyons, a landscape he sketched, painted, and described in awestruck tones in letters and diaries. Over the next three years Everett, an aspiring artist and poet, set off on several months-long rambles, often going weeks without speaking with another human being (though always keeping in touch with parents and friends back home through letters he mailed from remote trading posts, where he bought food and supplies). And then, during a 1934 trek, he simply vanished. Whether he committed suicide, died in an accidental fall, or was murdered by Native Americans or the local Mormon settlers has never been determined.

The Interest in Everett Ruess

In the years since, Everett has been taken up as a kind of patron saint of various lovers of the Southwest, from backpackers to New Agers to environmentalists. In a new book, veteran journalist David Roberts (who has written about Ruess for *National Geographic Adventure* magazine and elsewhere) seeks to replace hagiography with explanation; more than anything, he hopes to help solve what he calls "a riddle that has no parallel in the history of the American West."

Finding Everett Ruess: The Life and Unsolved Disappearance of a Legendary Wilderness Explorer is, weirdly, just one of three books about Ruess to come out in the past year. Last September [2010] saw the first paperback edition of *The Mystery of Everett Ruess*, edited by W.L. Rusho (the hardcover came out in 2002), and in late August [2011] *Everett Ruess: His Short Life, Mysterious Death, and Astonishing Afterlife*, by Philip L. Fradkin, will be published. The Roberts book features a foreword by Jon Krakauer, whose *Into the Wild* launched both his career and the cult following of Chris McCandless, another solitary young man who died alone in the wilderness.

Like McCandless, Ruess played around with pseudonyms and wrote at great length about his discomfort with urban life and modern civilization. Both inspire great admiration, among both kindred spirits (like Aron Ralston, the hiker who amputated his own arm and inspired the James Franco movie) and armchair explorers. I don't get them at all. While the mysterious nature of Ruess's disappearance (and assumed death) yields a great detective story as told by Roberts, the rest of it—especially the apparently huge population who not only admire but envy Ruess and McCandless and their lonely, dangerous, and ultimately deadly vision quests—just seems crazy to me.

Henry David Thoreau was an American author, poet, and naturalist who retreated to the woods near his home in Concord, Massachusetts, for two years and wrote about the experience in Walden, *published in 1854.* © Rühnert/picture-alliance/dpa/AP Images.

A Split Along Gender Lines

I don't think I'm alone. A highly unscientific inquiry (status update on my Facebook page) yielded a near-absolute split among my friends between those who think it sounds wonderful to travel solo through an unpeopled landscape (mostly men) and those who think it sounds boring, uncomfortable, terrifying, or just plain dumb (mostly women). Could this be about gender? There is, after all, a long history of solitude as a test or marker of true manhood—before Everett Ruess there was [writer and naturalist Henry David] Thoreau at Walden [Pond] (so what if he was less than a mile from his mother's house, to which he reportedly sent his laundry regularly), mountain men both real and imagined (Grizzly Adams, anyone?), and of course, Jesus' 40-day sojourn in the wilderness.

Thoreau is arguably the originator of the American myth of the solo man in the wilderness. He retreated to the woods for two years, a stretch of time he recounted in 1854's *Walden*. The picture he painted of self-sufficiency in *Walden* may be slightly exaggerated: He was less than a mile from home and frequently received meals and other comforts from his family and friends.

While the ranks of explorers includes some amazing women, real exploration typically involves great crews of people, from guides to porters to hunters to the dudes back in the city with the money. The male solo explorer isn't trying to discover anything except himself. And while I am a big fan of self-discovery, it just doesn't make sense to me to pursue it outside the ordinary avenues of therapy, art classes, and late-night drunken conversations with dear friends.

For the menfolk, though, apparently journeys into the center of their souls are best undertaken more or less alone (hence the man cave, invented, I guess, for those who don't wish to live in an actual cave like Ruess, but still want to carve out a space free from the incessant, harping demands of civilization, offspring, and spouses—but with a 72-inch TV and pool table). Women, especially those of us with husbands and kids, probably crave time alone more than any other demographic sector, but we seem to define "alone" differently—in my case, it means "without my husband and kids," not "in a place unsullied by other human beings."

A Focus on the Self

This isn't to say that only men revere Ruess. Plenty of women love his sweet, boy-band innocence, his unspoiled nearly virginal face. And fans of both genders admire his woodblock prints (which actually are pretty gorgeous) and his heartfelt, nature-worshipping poetry (which isn't).

The last stanza of his most well-known poem goes like this:

> Say that I starved, that I was lost and weary;
>
> That I was burned and blinded by the desert sun;
>
> Footsore, thirsty, sick with strange diseases;
>
> Lonely and wet and cold, but that I kept my dream!

Self-dramatizing, self-important, self-pitying—it reads like a Hallmark card written by [English poet Rudyard] Kipling. This isn't to say that Ruess wasn't at times lost and weary, burned and sun-blinded, but he chose his suffering. Writing as he tramped through some of the poorest, godforsaken settlements during the Depression, Ruess more or less ignored the privations of the local ranchers and Indian population, choosing instead to focus all of his sympathy on a more deserving subject: himself.

Ruess wrote not just poetry but hundreds of letters, some of them lyrical and ecstatic enough to end up on coffee mugs and wall hangings. Roberts argues that, with more time, Ruess might have joined John Muir among the masters of American nature writing. But it's hard to escape the feeling that his early death (and youthful beauty) account for much of the fervor fans feel for him. However ridiculous or reckless his treks seem to some of us, it's hard not to feel for a boy who might have grown out of his man cave, if he'd had the chance.

Into the "Wild": How a Film and an Essay Reflect Our Changed Ideas About Nature

Evan Eisenberg

Evan Eisenberg is author of The Ecology of Eden: An Inquiry into the Dream of Paradise and a New Vision of Our Role in Nature.

In the following viewpoint, Eisenberg argues that two recent popular views about the wilderness are dangerous. Eisenberg argues that both Into the Wild *(the book and the film) and a recent essay by a historian posit that we hold myths about the wilderness that ought to be abandoned: The former illustrates that it is a mistake to have an overly romantic view of wilderness and the latter contends that there is no such thing as wild nature. Eisenberg contends that abandoning our myths about the wilderness is itself dangerous because within these mythologies are the seeds of much-needed reverence for nature.*

Tires crunch snow, molars crunch popcorn, and I think: *Doesn't look so wild to me.*

The italics and teeth are mine; the tires belong to the pickup that drops off Chris McCandless at the end of the road at the start of *Into the Wild.*

Two Views of Wilderness

Sean Penn's powerful film is based on Jon Krakauer's 1996 best seller of the same name, which brilliantly pieced together the puzzle of a young man who walked into the Alaskan wilderness and (no spoiler alert necessary, I think) never walked out. Harrowing in spots, the book nonetheless came as balm to a nation eager to believe that its newly revived interest in nature was overdone and it should probably just kick back with a six-pack and relax. Equally soothing, for some, was an essay by historian William Cronon published the year before in the *New York Times Magazine*. Titled "The Trouble with Wilderness," it argued that wilderness is "a human creation," and a recent one; in the wild, there is no such thing. Nearly every hectare of nature has a human history; to idealize untouched nature is to evade that history. "As we gaze into the mirror [wilderness] holds up for us, we too easily imagine that what we behold is Nature when in fact we see the reflection of our own unexamined longings and desires."

Both Krakauer's book and Cronon's essay put a spike in the romantic notion of wilderness, but the spikes pointed in very different directions. Cronon said wilderness was not real. Krakauer said it was so real that it could kill you. The political upshot (with [politician and coauthor of *A Contract with the Earth*] Newt Gingrich doing much of the shooting) was the same: Neither a mirage nor a monster needs protection. Neither is worth seeking out. Consign [writers John] Muir, [Henry David] Thoreau, and Jack London if not to the flames then to the upper shelves, where they are less likely to lead environmentalists to foolish zeal or youngsters to a cold doom.

Close readings of Krakauer and Cronon would not yield such conclusions, but we are not a nation of close readers. We are a nation of watchers, which is why Penn's take on *Into the Wild* requires scrutiny. (We'll come back to Cronon later.) For Penn, the story is rich but fairly simple: a tale of heroic folly. Fleeing a bourgeois life that he feels (since learning of his father's bigamy) is a lie, McCandless (Emile Hirsch) takes to the road, lives on the edge, and finally walks into the Alaskan wild, all in search of his "true" life. In the wild, he discovers that life is with people; but then, by a trick of fate and hydrology, it is too late.

Transcendence in the Wilderness

With tight close-ups of well-cast faces, Penn's film lets us feel both the disgust that drove McCandless away from society and (for a far longer span) the love that, belatedly, calls him back. Penn fares less well with landscape. We see the southwestern desert, the rapids of the Colorado [River], the foothills of Denali [also known as Mount McKinley], places that enraptured McCandless; but in place of rapture we have establishing shots or travel footage of the sort that may beckon from the edge of this Web page. Even the Grand Canyon seems unremarkable until we meet a couple of backpackers from Copenhagen gleefully dispensing hot dogs. They are the scenic highlights, and not just because they're nearly naked.

Facescapes, by contrast, are traced as lovingly as if by a blind man's fingers. We walk out of the theater prepared to draw a topographical map of [actors] Hal Holbrook or Catherine Keener or even, God help us, Vince Vaughn. We walk out, strange to say, with our love of our neighbors restored. [Mockumentary character] Borat, groping for America's dark netherparts, instead revealed its open hand and patient heart. McCandless, fleeing his family, finds surrogate fathers, mothers, sisters, and brothers. He turns up saints under every rock, on every concrete slab.

Penn is reasonably faithful to his source but his few infidelities are telling. In the book, a 16-year-old gamine throws herself at McCandless but is mostly dodged. In the movie, the incident is inflated into a nascent romance, though a chaste one. This is done, I guess, partly for the obvious Hollywood reasons and partly to make the finish more conventionally tragic: not just a lost life (those are a dime a dozen) but a lost love. Penn also twists the knife by adopting the earliest, and first discarded, of Krakauer's three theories of how the young man died: the one that makes him seem most like a chump.

Krakauer, from his own experience as a rock climber, knows that wilderness can offer an escape from oppressive family relations. But he doesn't think that this makes the wilderness quest any less real. Transcendence is, by definition, transcendence of something; if that something happens to be tawdry, so much the better. McCandless embarked on a mythic quest in more or less the prescribed manner. He walked into the wild armed with gifts given him by mages encountered along the way. Of the many "uses" of wilderness, this is not the least. The outcome was tragic, but if that outcome had not been possible—had it not been possible for the dragon to slay him—the quest would have been a joke.

The Holy Man

Penn knows this, too. In interviews, he speaks of the need for rites of passage, absent or gelded or debased in our day. (My own involved a battle with inked sheepskin before a crowd of hungry primates, just after my 13th birthday.) Yet in the film he tends to play up his hero's folly. Oddly, this seems to be Penn's way of romanticizing him (perhaps in Penn's own image): making him both a tragic hero and a kind of holy fool.

Of course, the holy man, like the hero, must venture into the wilderness to find truth. Siddhartha, Zarathustra, Moses, Elijah, Mohammed, John the Baptist, Jesus: They all did it. But to extract truth from the wilderness, it helps to come out alive. Suppose Jesus had eaten some alkaloid-spiked seeds: A queasy crucifixion that would have been, and not much of a subject for [German Renaissance artist Lucas] Cranach or [German composer Johann Sebastian] Bach, especially as they would never have known who Jesus was. Yet, we know who McCandless was precisely because he *didn't* make it out alive.

"You're not Jesus, are you?" McCandless is asked—half-seriously in the book, half-jokingly in the film. Penn himself is dead serious: By the film's end, the iconography of the gaunt, bearded, agonized figure in the loincloth is hard to miss. "Who do you think you are, God?" Mom (Marcia Gay Harden) asks

Dad in a flashback that is not in the book. "I am God," Dad responds. (William Hurt, precise as ever, shows us that Dad is 82.3 percent joking.) Chris is thus the Son of God who dies for our sins—or, more to the point, for God's, which might well be said of the real Jesus, too.

Penn's mythologizing . . . is gripping, but troubling, too. For a case can be made that it was McCandless' need to see himself under the klieg light of myth, with little room for shade or nuance, that was his undoing. As Krakauer makes plain, but Penn (despite that scruffy, snow-crunching opening scene) does not, McCandless willed his wilderness to be wilder than it really was. In truth, he was never more than a few days' hike from a traveled road. The abandoned bus in which he made his camp sat just outside the boundary of the wilderness preserve. There were cabins (uninhabited at that time of year) five miles away. There was an abandoned cable-and-basket rig he could have used to cross the Teklanika River. There were points upstream that might well have been fordable even with the river in flood. He would have known about these things if he'd bought a USGS [United States Geological Survey] map. Of the magic gifts McCandless lacked, that would have been the cheapest and easiest to obtain.

Why didn't he get one? Krakauer has an answer: He yearned "to wander uncharted country, to find a blank spot on the map." But in 1992, there were no blank spots. So, "[h]e simply got rid of the map."

The Dangerous Myth

Here is where the spikes meet, where Cronon and Krakauer concur: The myth of wilderness can be dangerous, to the individual as well as to society as a whole. The problem is, the absence of that myth is more dangerous still.

Since Cronon's essay appeared, the scientific evidence has piled up on both sides of the scale. On the one hand, it has become clear that many places we think of as wild have in fact been transformed by millennia of human meddling. Even the Amazon rain forest owes its most fertile soil—the *terra preta* or "black earth," which is thought to map, in aggregate, an area the size of France—to Indian "cool burning." At the same time, it has become ever clearer that places we think of as wild—however imperfect their wildness—are crucial to human survival. They are so by virtue of the wildness that *is* in them: the ecological intelligence that has evolved over millions of years and will keep evolving if we don't pave it over. The flow of energy, the cycling of water and nutrients, the mix of gases in the atmosphere, the regulation of climate and of the oceans' salinity: These and other vital services are provided free of charge. We can, if we are modest and deft and clever, work in partnership with this intelligence, but we can never fully duplicate it, control it, or replace it with mechanisms of our own.

The Indians of the Amazon could live in wilderness, stretching and torquing it subtly without squeezing out its wildness. We can't. Our tools are too brutal and we swing them about too freely. Above all, there are too damned many of us. If we get too cozy with wilderness (or "wilderness")—if we convince ourselves that we are competent to manage or "garden" or "steward" every inch of the Earth's surface—we are asking for trouble. As I wrote some years back, wilderness is indeed a social construction, but so is the guard rail at the edge of a cliff.

The object Cronon tried, with some success, to dismantle is, for all its difficulties, one of immense value, both spiritual and practical. In order to have practical value, it must have spiritual value: a paradox, but true. Religion is constantly building fences, planting hedges, scarifying our soles for traction against the slippery slope. The trick, of course, is to respect the guard rail but remember that one may, from time to time, have to climb over it. When we read on the front page of the *New York Times* that the Nature Conservancy, in acquiring 161,000 acres of Adirondack wild lands, has gone into the logging business, we are right to be skeptical but not closed-minded. And when we walk into the wild ourselves, we are right to do so in fear and trembling, with our feet on the ground and a good, up-to-date map in our pack.

Into the Wild Has Led to Many Inexperienced Hikers Visiting the Alaska Wilderness

Tim Mowry

Tim Mowry is outdoors editor for the Fairbanks Daily News-Miner, *a daily newspaper in Fairbanks, Alaska.*

In the following viewpoint, Mowry contends that officials in Alaska have noticed an increase in the number of hikers on the Stampede Trail destined for the bus where Christopher McCandless died in 1992, as told in the book and movie Into the Wild. *Mowry reports that a Swiss woman drowned trying to cross the Teklanika River, the same river that had trapped McCandless, though it is unknown where the woman was headed. Mowry claims that officials say the Teklanika River is extremely dangerous to cross, and many inexpert hikers use a rope improperly, increasing their risk of death.*

The fact that a 29-year-old Swiss woman drowned Saturday [August 14, 2010] while attempting to cross the Teklanika River on the Stampede Trail doesn't surprise Jon Nierenberg.

What surprises him is that it didn't happen to someone a lot sooner.

The Impact of *Into the Wild*

Nierenberg, who owns a lodge four miles from the end of Stampede Road, said it was just a matter of time before someone drowned trying to cross the river to reach the old Fairbanks city bus made famous in the movie *Into the Wild*.

Since the critically acclaimed film was released three years ago, the bus where 24-year-old Chris McCandless starved to death in 1992 has become a destination for adventurers following in McCandless' footsteps.

"Honestly, I'm amazed this hasn't happened earlier," Nierenberg said Monday by phone.

Whether or not backpacker Claire Jane Ackermann was on her way to the bus is not known, but Nierenberg said practically everyone who hikes the Stampede Trail has the same destination in mind.

"It's not a casual place to go hiking," Nierenberg said. "I have absolutely no doubt what she was doing out there."

Ackermann was trying to wade east to west across the swollen stream with a 27-year-old man from France about 1 p.m. Saturday. The pair was headed in the direction of the bus. The two hikers had tied themselves onto a rope that had been placed across the stream earlier this summer. They lost their footing and were pulled under by the current.

The man told Alaska State Troopers and rangers from Denali National Park and Preserve that he was able to cut himself free from the main line and make his way to the bank, where he dropped his backpack. When he turned back, the man said, Ackermann was underwater.

The hiker made his way back and cut her loose from the main line. He floated downstream with her for half a mile. When the man pulled her to shore, Ackermann was unresponsive. The man tried to resuscitate her but was unsuccessful.

The French hiker ran into another hiking party, which reported the incident to troopers and the National Park Service. Ackermann's body and the French hiker were flown out by a park helicopter Saturday evening.

Hikers Bound for McCandless' Bus

Troopers spokeswoman Megan Peters said a trooper asked the French man whether they were hiking to the old green-and-white bus. "He said 'no,'" Peters said. "He said they were just hiking in the area."

"It's anybody's guess what they were doing out there," she said.

The bus, located about 18 miles from the end of Stampede Road off the [George] Parks Highway in Healy, has become a destination for people from around the world since Jon Krakauer wrote his best-selling book *Into the Wild* in 1996. After the book was adapted into a critically acclaimed film starring Emile Hirsch and directed by Sean Penn three years ago, the number of hikers trying to reach the bus increased significantly.

Troopers and park service rangers have conducted several search and rescues involving hikers who have become lost or stranded while hiking to the bus in the last few years.

A month ago, troopers rescued four teenagers who became stranded on their way to the abandoned bus. The teens, ages 16 and 17, got separated after their vehicle became stuck on Stampede Trail. The teens were found by a Fairbanks trooper in a Super Cub [small aircraft] and a Cantwell trooper on an ATV [all-terrain vehicle].

"Everybody has noticed an increase (in the number of hikers going to the bus) in the last three years," said Richard Moore, north district ranger for Denali National Park and Preserve. There is "general concern" because many of the people hiking to the bus are inexperienced in the Alaska back-country, he said.

"We try to give information to people and tell them that they should be prepared and educated about how to travel in the backcountry," Moore said.

The Teklanika River in Alaska has been an obstacle for many hikers attempting to reach the bus where Christopher McCandless's remains were found in 1992. In August 2010, a Swiss hiker drowned in an attempt to cross the swollen river. © Accent Alaska.com / Alamy.

The Dangerous River Crossing

The Stampede Trail river crossing is along the park's northern boundary and park rangers are still trying to determine if Ackermann drowned inside or outside of the park. She was about a half mile inside the park boundary when she was brought to shore by her companion.

The Teklanika River, about 10 miles from the end of Stampede Road, poses the biggest challenge—and threat—for hikers on the Stampede Trail. The swift, glacier-fed stream is difficult to cross even at low water.

On Saturday, the river was raging because of glacial melting in the warm temperatures, park spokesperson Kris Fister said.

A week and a half ago, two hikers called Nierenberg on their satellite phone when they couldn't get back across the river after hiking to the bus.

Nierenberg told them they could wade upstream to look for a better place to cross or wait until early morning to cross when the water was at its lowest point. He also gave them the phone number for Era Aviation to call for a helicopter if they wanted to spend the $1,000 or so that would cost.

As it turned out, the two hikers met three others, and the group was able to cross.

For whatever reason, Nierenberg said, he has seen an increase in the amount of bus traffic this summer. Some of the hikers stop at his lodge to talk about the trail and river crossing, but most of them don't, he said. The ones that stop usually don't have a clue what they're doing, Nierenberg said.

"Most of these guys don't have any concept of river crossings," he said. "Most of their knowledge is from YouTube."

The Use of Rope to Cross the River

The rope across the river, which is still in place, appears to be about 3/8-inch braided, nylon rope and is tied on both ends to small trees and brush, said Moore, who has seen pictures. A rope across the river is not uncommon, the ranger said.

"Every time I've gone out there, someone has put up a rope somewhere across the river," he said. "It either gets broken or taken down or disappears in the winter."

Using a rope as a crossing aid is risky, Moore said.

"If properly used, it could help, but unfortunately a lot of people don't use it properly, and it leads to incidents like we had Saturday," he said.

Most people bring rope to help get them across the river, Nierenberg said. A former park ranger in Denali, Nierenberg said he was trained to cross rivers using walking sticks or a pole pointed upstream held by multiple people.

"Some of these guys are talking about crossing with rope tied around their waist, which is like suicide," he said.

A rope, he said, "is like tying yourself into a raft in Whitewater—it can help you live or it can help you die."

Nierenberg speculated that a group of five motorcyclists from the Lower 48 [referring to the contiguous United States], who hiked to the bus about three weeks ago, installed the rope. One of the motorcyclists was nearly swept downriver after getting knocked off his feet on the way back, he said.

"He was holding onto the rope and ended up having to let go," said Nierenberg, who talked to the men before they left and when they returned. "His friends ran downstream and fished him out.

"When he came back here his eyes were pretty wide," Nierenberg said. "He knew that he had almost died."

Rangers are still trying to determine whether the rope is inside or outside the park boundary, Moore said.

"Our best guess is one side may be in the park and the other side may not be in the park," he said.

If the rope is inside the park, Moore said, rangers will remove it. If the rope is on state land, he said, rangers will notify troopers.

What action troopers might take is unclear, Peters said.

"I think we will have to await word from the rangers before that would be assessed," she wrote in an e-mail. "I don't know if that would be an appropriate use of our resources, as it would have to be decided if it was an immediate threat to public safety."

For Further Discussion

1. Drawing upon the biographies of Jon Krakauer in Chapter 1, name three ways in which his mountain climbing has influenced his writing.

2. Several authors in Chapter 2 argue that Krakauer paints a sympathetic portrait of Christopher McCandless in *Into the Wild*. Do you agree? Why, or why not?

3. Dick Staub compares Christopher McCandless to Jack Kerouac and argues that both undertook adventures of a spiritual nature. Assuming McCandless's journey was of a spiritual nature, should this soften the censure and disapproval expressed against him? Addressing the critiques from at least two other authors in Chapter 2, explain your answer.

4. Stacy Taniguchi argues that adventure in the wilderness offers a path to self-actualization. He also recounts several stories in which both he and others came close to death through their adventures. Is risking death admirable in this way? Or is there something abhorrent about purposely putting one's self in harm's way? Explain your reasoning.

For Further Reading

Philip L. Fradkin, *Everett Ruess: His Short Life, Mysterious Death, and Astonishing Afterlife*. Berkeley: University of California Press, 2011.

Sam Keith from the journals and photo collections of Richard Proenneke, *One Man's Wilderness: An Alaskan Odyssey*. Anchorage: Alaska Northwest, 1973.

Jon Krakauer, *Eiger Dreams: Ventures Among Men and Mountains*. New York: Lyons & Burford, 1990.

————, *Into Thin Air: A Personal Account of the Mt. Everest Disaster*. New York: Villard, 1997.

————, *Three Cups of Deceit: How Greg Mortenson, Humanitarian Hero, Lost His Way*. New York: Anchor Books, 2011.

————, *Under the Banner of Heaven: A Story of Violent Faith*. New York: Random House, 2003.

————, *Where Men Win Glory: The Odyssey of Pat Tillman*. New York: Anchor Books, 2009.

Lloyd L. Morain, *The Human Cougar*. Buffalo, NY: Prometheus Books, 1976.

John Muir, *A Thousand-Mile Walk to the Gulf*. Boston: Houghton Mifflin, 1916.

David Roberts, *Finding Everett Ruess: The Life and Unsolved Disappearance of a Legendary Wilderness Explorer*. New York: Broadway Books, 2011.

W.L. Rusho, *The Mystery of Everett Ruess*. Layton, UT: Gibbs Smith, 2010.

Bibliography

Books

Richard Bangs   *The Lost River: A Memoir of Life, Death, and Transformation on Wild Water.* San Francisco, CA: Sierra Club Books, 2001.

James Campbell   *The Final Frontiersman: Heimo Korth and His Family, Alone in Alaska's Arctic Wilderness.* New York: Atria Books, 2005.

James Oliver Curwood   *The Wolf Hunters: A Tale of Adventure in the Wilderness.* New York: Grossett & Dunlap, 1908.

Tony Horwitz, ed.   *The Devil May Care: Fifty Intrepid Americans and Their Quest for the Unknown.* New York: Oxford University Press, 2003.

Tom Kizzia   *Pilgrim's Wilderness: A True Story of Faith and Madness on the Alaska Frontier.* New York: Crown, 2013.

Robert Kull   *Solitude: Seeking Wisdom in Extremes: A Year Alone in the Patagonia Wilderness.* Novato, CA: New World Library, 2008.

Anne LaBastille   *Woodswoman: Living Alone in the Adirondack Wilderness.* New York: E.P. Dutton, 1978.

John Muir — *The Wilderness World of John Muir.* Ed. Edwin Way Teale. Boston: Houghton Mifflin, 1954.

Roderick Frazier Nash — *Wilderness and the American Mind,* 4th ed. New Haven, CT: Yale University Press, 2001.

Anne Purdy, as told to Robert Specht — *Tisha: The Story of a Young Teacher in the Alaska Wilderness.* New York: St. Martin's Press, 1976.

Cheryl Strayed — *Wild: From Lost to Found on the Pacific Crest Trail.* New York: Vintage, 2013.

Scott P. Werther — *Jon Krakauer's Adventure on Mt. Everest.* New York: Children's Press, 2002.

Periodicals

Chip Brown — "I Now Walk into the Wild," *New Yorker,* February 8, 1993.

Ellen Charles — "Into the Wild," *Mother Jones,* September 28, 2007.

Darcy Courteau — "Call of the Wild: Community and Solitude in the Alaskan Wilderness," *Atlantic,* May 2012.

David Denby — "Lost Men," *New Yorker,* October 8, 2007.

Timothy Egan — "At Home With: Jon Krakauer; Back from Everest, Haunted," *New York Times,* May 23, 1996.

Malcolm Jones   "Murder in the Name of God: Best-Selling Journalist Jon Krakauer Finds Religion—in a 1984 Double Homicide," *Newsweek*, July 21, 2003.

Christopher Keyes   "'I Want This Movie to Grip People in the Heart,'" *Outside*, August 27, 2007.

Jon Krakauer   "Death of an Innocent," *Outside*, January 1993.

Jon Krakauer   "How Chris McCandless Died," *New Yorker*, September 12, 2013.

Jon Krakauer   "The Toll You Pay to Enter This Eden Is Sweat, Pain and Fear," *Smithsonian*, June 1995.

Kevin Lally   "Into the Wild," *Film Journal International*, October 2007.

Lou Lumenick   "Dead Man Camping," *New York Post*, September 21, 2007.

Jonah Raskin   "Kings of the Road," *Nation*, July 30, 2007.

R.R. Reno   "The End of the Road," *First Things*, October 2008.

Jack Ryan   "Into the Wild," *Aethlon: The Journal of Sport Literature*, Fall–Winter 2008.

Sura Wood   "Into the Wild," *Hollywood Reporter*, August 30, 2007.

Index

CPSIA information can be obtained
at www.ICGtesting.com
Printed in the USA
FFOW04n2055280815
16441FF